*The
Restless
Woman*

The Restless Woman

Beverly LaHaye

Zondervan Publishing House
Grand Rapids, Michigan

THE RESTLESS WOMAN
Copyright © 1984 by The Zondervan Corporation
Grand Rapids, Michigan

Zondervan Books are published by Zondervan
Publishing House, 1415 Lake Drive, S.E.,
Grand Rapids, Michigan 49506

Library of Congress Cataloging in Publication Data
LaHaye, Beverly.
    The restless woman.
      "A Zondervan book"—T.p. verso. Includes bibliographies.
      1. Woman (Christian theology)   2. Feminism—Religious aspects—
Christianity—Controversial literature.   I. Title.
BT704.L345   1984   261.8'344   84-13097
ISBN 0-310-27091-X

Designed by Ann Cherryman

Printed in the United States of America

87 88 89 90 91 92 93 / EP / 11 10 9 8 7 6 5 4 3

CONTENTS

Acknowledgments

A published book is never the effort of a single person, and this one is no exception. Therefore I would like to express my heartfelt thanks to several who helped me complete this project.

The encouragement my husband Tim gave me kept me going. After beginning the book I developed some physical problems that delayed my research and hindered my creativity. Tim patiently prayed me through.

Frank York provided great assistance as a resource person. He has the gift of dependability and is dedicated to God and country. This book would not have been completed without him.

My dear friend Glorya Hammers did some volunteer research for me. Michael Jameson, my CWA research assistant, added his efforts to this book, and my faithful sister, Barrie Lyons, a college English instructor, gave her touch to make it readable.

Of no less value were the prayers of many who promised to pray for me as the book progressed, lest I lose patience and develop a restlessness of my own.

Preface

It took a long time to write this book. It was completed some two years after I intended, because I set it aside when Tim and I realized that the Lord was leading us to launch our weekly television show, "The LaHayes on Family Life." The demands placed on us in producing this program, a busy traveling schedule holding Family Life Seminars all over America, my involvement as president of Concerned Women for America (assisting it to grow into one of the important voices for Christian women on family and women's issues) all delayed my writing this book. However, during that time the subject was ripening and growing in my heart and perhaps had a chance to develop and mature more completely.

In the meantime I have become more aware of different ways that restlessness reveals itself. I am reminded of the father who wrote to me regarding his unwed, pregnant teenaged daughter. He related how she had been so restless during her sophomore year in high school, and now, one year later, she was expecting a child. Her restlessness seemed to be a result of a rebellious heart that eventually led her into many sins.

Recently I was waiting in the Dallas airport for my plane connection when a father with two children sat down near me. The children were darling little blonds with big blue eyes. As cute as they were, there seemed to be an atmosphere of insecurity and sadness surrounding them. I began to talk to the children, and soon the father entered the conversation. My natural question to them was something like "Where is your mother?" I learned that the wife and mother had become disillusioned with mothering and homemaking, and her discontentment grew into wanting something more or different. In her restless state she decided to dump the homemaking and mothering onto someone else so she could pursue what she wanted to do. She had decided that she needed a career of her own. His eyes moist, a child at each hand, this young father told me that he loved his wife, but she had walked out on him and the two kids to "find herself" and develop *her* personal desires. Restlessness and selfishness often go hand in hand.

The stories keep coming to me and letters continue to arrive on my desk relating how the restlessness of individuals can eventually destroy a life or a family. The sad stories of hurting people and destroyed families motivated me to try to help these people through writing.

In a sense, *The Restless Woman* is a sequel to my earlier book, *I Am a Woman By God's Design*. In *I Am a Woman,* I presented what I believe is God's perfect plan for women as individuals, wives, and mothers. But I did not deal specifically with the "restless woman" in American society.

Who is the restless woman? She's a woman who has been "liberated" from traditional moral standards, yet now finds herself feeling empty and without goals; she's the suburban housewife whose children are in school all day; she's the Christian mother caring for her young who feels as though she's not contributing enough to the work of the church; she's the young educated woman who has become a mother, yet feels unchallenged at home; she's the so-called liberated woman who has demanded the right to control her own body and has ultimately snuffed out the life of another human being; she's the radical feminist who is determined to restructure our society according to her vision of utopia.

Restlessness is usually influenced by excess pressure—whether it be financial instability, the lack of self-worth or fulfillment, the gnawing pressure caused by greed or demanding selfish rights, or having one's priorities distorted and out of focus. These are not problems identified with just feminist women. In essence, the restless woman is *any* woman who is uneasy and dissatisfied with her lot in life. She feels hollow—filled with anxiety—desolate within her spirit. She has few answers, but plenty of questions about her reason for existence. She questions her personal fulfillment and struggles like a butterfly trying to break out of the cocoon. In her relentless quest for "happiness" or personal fulfillment, she grows more discontent. She often feels as if she's chasing a mirage in the desert. The closer she seems to get to her goal of satisfaction, the more distant it becomes.

In writing this book, I have attempted to take an honest look at the restless woman—to discover some of the roots of her discontent and suggest ways out of her dilemma.

1.

Why Talk About Restlessness?

While traveling across the country on a major airline, a flight attendant and I were discussing some of the dramatic changes in the attitudes of people, especially women. She told me she had been flying for fifteen years and had never been physically attacked by a passenger until recently.

Apparently a female traveler had become irritated over some discussion while in flight and her voice rose in pitch and volume. When the flight attendant went to check on the situation, the passenger stood in the aisle, picked up the flight attendant bodily, and threw her into the beverage cart. That outburst was not the result of instant anger, but the culmination of long periods of restlessness. The passenger's action resembles a slow cooker suddenly becoming pressurized to the point of explosion.

Admittedly this incident is rather unusual, but there is a growing restlessness among some women and I see it demonstrated in the midst of pressure as never before. The encouraging note in this violent display of anger was the reaction of the other passengers. Their sympathy was directed toward the flight attendant, and the female passenger's bad manners were condemned.

Few of us have seen or felt that kind of female

brutality or feeble attempts to be "macho." But most of us have observed or been the victims of women who showed their restlessness by being short-tempered, exploding with angry words, or reflecting little femininity.

There has been an obvious deterioration in the actions and manners of women in general. Fortunately there are still females who believe in womanhood with dignity and respect for proper manners, dress, and vocabulary. This decline has not been sudden, but a gradual change that has caused many men to no longer hold doors for ladies, to give their seats to standing ladies, or to guard vocabulary in the presence of ladies.

Many years ago women began smoking in public. Women first developed a new image as glamorous smokers (a profitable boost to cigarette sales in America), then they were seen in bars. Gradually they competitively shared dirty stories and became aggressive sexually.

Were these behavioral changes growing evidence of the restless spirit in women? Did women want to enter the world of men and become macho feminists? As modest vocabulary and actions drastically changed, demands came for job equality. All jobs, even rugged and dangerous ones, were to be made available to women.

What was happening to families while all these changes were taking place? Where were the wives and mothers who give the foundation to home life? What happened to the priorities of training and raising children to become productive adults? Where were the fathers to lead the homes and support the wives in this significant responsibility?

In the midst of this growing restlessness among women, families were beginning to hurt and were struggling to remain together. Juvenile rebellion began to increase; thousands of children were running away from home; the climbing divorce rate became almost unchartable. The rapidly increasing drug abuse, teenage suicides, sexual promiscuity, and the murder of thousands of unborn babies are indicative of the serious problems facing the American family.

THE LAST DAYS

Today we are living in a fast-paced, highly complex society where moral values and marriages are discarded as easily as the morning newspaper. As a result, many American families are filled with confusion and unhappiness.

I am not surprised by all of this, because I believe we are living in the final days of history prior to the return of Jesus Christ to establish His kingdom on earth.

The apostle Paul gave us a detailed description of how men and women would be treating one another in the last days. In 2 Timothy 3:1–5, Paul told Timothy, "But mark this: There will be terrible times in the last days. People will be lovers of themselves, lovers of money, boastful, proud, abusive, disobedient to their parents, ungrateful, unholy, without love, unforgiving, slanderous, without self-control, brutal, not lovers of the good, treacherous, rash, conceited, lovers of pleasure rather than lovers of God—having a form of godliness but denying its power. Have nothing to do with them."

In Romans 1:26–32, Paul also describes the hardened hearts of those who have continually rejected the love of God. There is a point at which God simply gives them over to their own perversions. Paul says, "Because of this, God gave them over to shameful lusts. Even their women exchanged natural relations for unnatural ones. In the same way the men also abandoned natural relations with women and were inflamed with lust for one another. Men committed indecent acts with other men, and received in themselves the due penalty for their perversion" (vv. 26–28).

Paul's descriptions fit twentieth-century America. He is describing an age characterized by an obsession with "self"—self-fulfillment, selfish ambition, self-centeredness. Men and women, filled with intellectual pride, are rebelling against authority. We should not be surprised to find many restless, unhappy women in a country filled with many insolent, proud, deceitful, immoral, and merciless people.

Just a little more than thirty years ago, Americans generally adhered to Judeo-Christian morality. Although we might have disagreed on matters of Bible doctrine, we agreed on basic moral principles. We believed in the necessity of such virtues as truth, fidelity, thrift, honesty, and chastity. But today our land is divided into hundreds of subcultures, many claiming the right to pursue and achieve their own selfish interests—with no regard for the long-term effects on civilization.

"Doing your own thing" has been lifted to the level of a theological truth or constitutional right. For many it seems to matter little that "doing your own thing" is bringing about the destruction of society.

HUMANISM AND THE MORAL REVOLUTION

The mass communications media has wrought moral revolution. The revolution has brought with it discontentment and social destruction. Newspapers, magazines, television, movies, and radio have been used by secular humanists to tear down traditional standards of morality in our nation.

With the fading of Christian morality, secular humanists seek to impose their own moral code upon all Americans. One of the key teachings in humanism is that men and women are "self-autonomous"—meaning we are all a "law unto ourselves." Moreover, humanists believe that God is a myth and that we must construct our own morality. To seek "the good life" is the highest calling we have.

The allure of humanistic thinking is most evident in *Playboy* magazine, founded by Hugh Hefner in 1953. In his hedonistic "Playboy Philosophy" Hefner suggests that both men and women should seek unrestrained pleasure. There is no place for faithfulness in marriage;

no room for commitment, children, or true love. There is only an endless series of casual sexual encounters, drug and alcohol abuse, materialism, and intellectual pride.

Unfortunately the "Playboy Philosophy" has become the unconscious motivating force in the lives of millions of men and women. As a result of this relentless pursuit of pleasure and self-fulfillment, our whole culture is in danger of being destroyed. Nearly half of the marriages in America now end in divorce, leaving the potential for millions of psychologically damaged children. More than a million children flee from their homes each year, and many end up selling their bodies on street corners. Herpes venereal disease has afflicted over twenty million Americans, and AIDS disease is threatening to infect thousands of transfusions. More than a million babies are murdered each year in abortions; and the pornography empire reaps more than $5 billion a year by sexually exploiting women and children.

THE RESTLESS WOMAN

Because of humanist attacks on the traditional family, and because of inflation and other economic pressures, it has become increasingly confusing to be a woman in the 1980s. Women are being torn apart emotionally as they struggle to find their identities. Their natural maternal instincts are in constant conflict with what the feminists are telling them. Liberated women like Helen Gurley Brown tell women that they "can have it all." But millions of women are discovering that it's simply not possible. One successful young television executive told feminist leader Betty Friedan, "I know I'm lucky to have this job, but you people who fought for these things had your families. You already had your men and children. What are we supposed to do?"[1]

Many men and women are in a state of anxiety over their social and sexual roles. The restlessness in women is being caused by both real and manufactured problems. Inflation has forced many women into the work world, but this has not brought them liberation and personal satisfaction. It has simply added to an already hectic schedule.

The blurring of sexual distinctions in our society is being applauded by the feminists as a victory for equality. But the price we are paying for this equalizing of sexual roles is far too high—the breakup of families.

Ultimately society as a whole is going to suffer from broken marriages. Have you considered that your relationship with your spouse and children *inevitably* affects your friends, your church, your community, and the nation?

Your private "sins" against your family negatively affect the community around you. If you divorce your husband, you are putting undue pressure on others to pick up the pieces of your broken relationship: divorce courts, juvenile authorities, social workers, pastors, daycare centers, and many others must share the burden of your divorce.

If you have children, you may discover—too late— the psychological damage that has been done to them. These children suffer irreparable harm unless the Lord heals them.

Dr. Harold M. Voth, author of *The Castrated Family,* is a psychoanalyst at the famous Menninger Clinic in Topeka, Kansas. He has treated thousands of patients suffering from psychological illnesses. He observes, "The cycle of sick or weak people who are the product of sick or broken families keeps repeating itself, the effects spread from one generation to the next and slowly but surely the sickness tears down the best traditions of mankind which made our society strong."[2] Men and women who are discontent within their marriage relationships must realize that more is involved than their own feelings or desires.

The Family and Restlessness

Sociologists and theologians recognize that the family is the basic social unit. Within the family each member finds love, affection, and moral values. He develops a sense of identity and is trained to become a responsible member of society. When the family unit breaks down, the entire society will eventually crumble.

Within the family, the mother and father have mutually dependent roles to fulfill. The father is the provider, protector, and disciplinarian. The mother is the keeper of the home (the homemaker), whose primary role is to meet the physical needs of her family and to give the children love, guidance, direction, and security. Ideally there should be an interdependence between the mother and father and a division of labor founded on love and respect.

It is my firm belief, based on the study of God's Word (Eph. 5:23), that the man is to take his place as the head or leader of the family. But his leadership is to be based on the lordship of Jesus Christ in his own life. He is to be merciful, compassionate, and loving. He is also to be firm and responsible in his treatment of his wife and children.

When a man fails to lead his family, or when the woman usurps control of the family, untold damage is done to that family unit.

Dr. Voth notes, "Childhood experiences within the family, and their subsequent effects, have been implicated in all of the psychiatric illnesses (psychoses and neuroses), personality disorders, perversions, homosexuality, transsexuality, transvestism, drug addiction, alcoholism, delinquency, suicide, crime, the current blurring of sex roles (which is becoming widespread at an alarming rate), child abuse, divorce, and failure to adapt to life generally or in specific instances."[3]

The restlessness we see in women (and in men, too) can only result in ruining families and destroying society. But are there any solutions?

Love Is the Key

There is no way that a scientist can measure love. It's an intangible substance that defies scientific explanation. Yet love is as real as the wind and as necessary for a healthy life as water and air. It is the most important element in any human relationship, but it is especially vital within marriage. Love is an act of our will and the most powerful force in the universe.

The Bible tells us that God, our Creator, loved the world. He loved you and me so much that He sent Jesus Christ into the world to die for our sins. Jesus, God incarnate, lived a perfect life and yet was nailed to a cross to redeem us from the curse of sin. Jesus loved us so much He willingly suffered death for us.

This kind of sacrificial, unconditional love must be present in a marriage. In 1 Corinthians 13, Paul tells us the attributes of love. "If I speak in the tongues of men and of angels, but have not love, I am only a resounding gong or a clanging cymbal. . . . Love is patient, love is kind. It does not envy, it does not boast, it is not proud. It is not rude, it is not self-seeking, it is not easily angered, it keeps no record of wrongs. Love does not delight in evil but rejoices with the truth. It always protects, always trusts, always hopes, always perseveres" (vv. 1–7).

Love is more than a fluttery feeling in your chest when you first fall in love. It is not the degraded lust that so often passes for love in the world today. Love is not a combination of chemical reactions in your brain; nor is it an imbalance in your hormone levels—although those are affected. Real love is a healing, energizing force in our lives that can transform others.

Whether we live in civilized or uncivilized cultures, whether we're rich or poor, young or old, we must have love to survive. The lack of love, whether to be given or to be received, can cause us to think and act in unstable and inconsiderate ways. To love and to be loved gives humans balanced and wholesome attitudes toward life.

The Choice Is Ours

On the other hand, there is power in hatred. Hatred can destroy those around us; it can ruin relationships and ultimately destroy peace and joy. Hatred brings forth anguish, fear, disgust, isolation, and spiritual death.

I believe that God has given us a free will. We are free to choose to love or to hate. It is our decision. No matter what we choose, we reap the consequences of our choices. It is a real tragedy that many men and women have chosen to live lives filled with hate—hatred against a particular race or class; hatred against an economic system; hatred against men or women; hatred against individuals.

Feminism and Hatred

In 1947 Ferdinand Lundberg, a journalist, and Dr. Marynia F. Farnham, a psychiatrist, published the book *Modern Woman, The Lost Sex*. In this classic work they reviewed the historical roots of the feminist movement and showed how destructive it has been to male and female relationships.

These authors believe that much of the restlessness, neuroses, and unhappiness found in women have their roots in the philosophies of modern totalitarian movements: socialism and communism, anarchism, nihilism, anarcho-syndicalism, feminism, anti-Semitism, and "pseudo-biologic racism." All these movements, including feminism, are based on "...hatred, hostility, and violence."[4]

Lundberg and Farnham observe that most of the radical leaders of these revolutionary movements were simply seeking personal power and ego gratification. Many of them were subconsciously rebelling against parental authority.

Mary Wollenstonecraft, a radical feminist philosopher of the eighteenth century, is a tragic example of what can happen to a woman who has been treated cruelly by her father. In a later chapter I will go into more detail about how her disrupted family life has negatively affected our whole culture.

GOD'S IMMUTABLE LAWS

My husband and I have based our ministry and lives upon the unchangeable truths of the Bible. We believe God created an orderly world, and if we obey His commands, we will be well-adjusted, happy, and prosperous.

Some feminists, however, reject the reality of God in their lives. In their efforts to restructure society, they are rebelling against the immutable laws of God. God, the author of all creation, rules over both the physical and moral laws of the universe. We cannot violate the physical laws of the universe without suffering permanent harm. No matter how much you might refuse to believe in the reality of gravity, if you step off the top of a skyscraper, you will inevitably fall to the sidewalk and perish. All the way down you may scream about your "rights" and frantically shout about your unbelief in gravity, but you will still fall ... and die. The same is true of God's moral laws. History is strewn with the debris of civilizations that violated God's moral laws. In the Bible God sets down specific rules for us to follow if we are to have healthful, wholesome relationships with those around us.

God's principles work. If we obey them, we will live happy lives; if we choose to disobey, we will end up living in terror and futility until the day we die. Jesus said it simply in Luke 11:28: "Blessed rather are those who hear the word of God and obey it." The laws of God apply equally to all cultures and every period of history. God does not discriminate against any race or people.

Think for a moment how much needless heartache and turmoil could be eliminated from our world if we just obeyed *one* of the Lord's teachings—His teaching on *adultery*. In Matthew 5:27–28, Jesus said, "You have heard that it was said, 'Do not commit adultery.' But I tell you that anyone who looks at a woman lustfully has already committed adultery with her in his heart."

If that one teaching were obeyed by men and women,

we would not have skyrocketing divorce rates, illegitimate children, and rampant venereal disease.

The radical feminists and playboys reject God's rule in their lives. They are determined to construct a humanistic utopia—a utopia in absolute violation of God's unchangeable laws. They don't realize the hell on earth they will be creating if they succeed in eradicating Christian morality from the world.

Male and Female...

God purposely created male and female with different physical and psychological characteristics. In the Book of Genesis we read that God created man first, then created woman *out of* and *for* man. Woman was fashioned to be a companion and a helper to man. God created men and women with complementary skills and thinking processes. In the marriage relationship, the husband and wife are to be "one flesh," working in cooperation to hold the family together.

In secular sociological and anthropological circles there are few who believe in God. As a result, these scientists can only theorize about the differences between men and women and about the reasons for the existence of the family structure.

Two viewpoints that sociologists and anthropologists use to explain human behavior are (1) cultural determinism and (2) biological determinism. The cultural determinists believe that training within the family or community determines what roles men and women are to play in the culture. They believe that the genetic makeup of men and women has little to do with role differentiation. Biological determinists, on the other hand, assert that genetic makeup plays a large part in determining male and female skills and attitudes.

Radical feminists firmly believe that all sexual roles are determined by cultural conditioning and have no biological basis. As a consequence of this erroneous belief, they feel they must transform our free enterprise system into a socialist and unisex society where all distinctions between men and women will be erased.

Their efforts have produced an alarming trend: masculinized women and feminized men. Some of the most extreme lesbian groups are actually setting up sperm banks in order to eliminate the need for heterosexual intercourse in their new society.

It is my belief that God has ordained certain relationships and responsibilities for males and females. If the feminists succeed in upsetting God's order, the result will be chaos and misery for the entire civilization. In a later chapter I'll be discussing the differences between males and females and their roles.

Restlessness and God's Word

Proverbs is one of the most practical, down-to-earth books in the Bible because it contains so much distilled wisdom. Proverbs 4:23–24 issues a warning to us: "Above all else, guard your heart, for it is the wellspring of life. Put away perversity from your mouth; keep corrupt talk far from your lips." It's easy to be taken in by what the world calls "wisdom," which in fact is nothing but foolishness to God. Our lives are shaped by what we see, read, and hear. Much of what comes to us through the mass media is designed to create feelings of ungratefulness and restlessness in our lives.

Women are especially vulnerable to this propaganda. Women's magazines like *Cosmopolitan, Self, Working Woman,* and others are sowing seeds of discontent. These magazines often ridicule and downgrade the importance of being a traditional wife and mother. The woman who stays at home and raises godly children is made to feel worthless and foolish.

Yet the truth is that the traditional mother is nurturing the future leaders of America in her home. What she does, or fails to do, for her children will affect future generations. The traditional woman must heed the words of Paul in Philippians 4:8. He says we should fill our minds with "whatever is true, whatever is right, whatever is pure, whatever is lovely, whatever is admirable—if anything is excellent or praiseworthy—think about such things."

WHY IS THIS BOOK NEEDED?

My prayer is that this book will clear up a great deal of confusion over what the proper role of a woman should be in the family, the church, and the community.

It is also my hope that those feminists who have been mistreated by husbands, fathers, or lovers will read this and discover that there is someone who loves them more than they could ever imagine—Jesus Christ. He alone has the power to heal the deep wounds many ardent feminists have suffered at the hands of men, and He alone can give them the love, peace, and contentment they never had as children. He is alive, waiting to help them. Instead of rejecting Jesus Christ, they need to receive Him by inviting Him into their hearts to become the Lord and Savior of their lives. His Word will teach us how to love and how to be lovely.

NOTES

[1] Betty Friedan, *The Second Stage* (New York: Summit Books, 1981), 16.

[2] Harold M. Voth, *The Castrated Family* (Kansas City, Mo.: Universal Press Syndicate, 1977), xiii.

[3] Ibid., 6.

[4] Ferdinand Lundberg and Marynia F. Farnham, *Modern Woman: The Lost Sex* (New York: Harper Brothers, 1947), 25.

2.

The Early Church and
Its Treatment of Women

We can better understand how God views the relationships between men and women by looking at the life of Jesus. How did He treat women? Did He put them down? Did He criticize them or shun them? Did He follow the rabbinical practice of the day by refusing to speak to women in public? Or did He attempt to break through the long-standing traditions in His dealing with women?

The fact is, Jesus is the ideal model of how *all* men are *supposed* to relate to women.

JESUS AND THE JEWISH WORLD

Jesus of Nazareth was born into a Jewish culture that had fallen away from the worship of the one true God. The forms of religion were still evident, but the religious leaders of the day were, by and large, hypocrites who enjoyed their position of influence and adulation in the community.

These men loved to walk through the marketplaces discussing theology, but inside they were spiritually dead. They had become "legalists" who were more concerned about the letter of the law than ministering to the spiritual needs and growth of the Jewish people.

Throughout the Gospels Jesus treated the Pharisees, Sadducees, and scribes more harshly than He did the most hardened sinner. He knew that these religious leaders had corrupted the laws of God by putting unbearable, unreasonable restrictions on the people. In their attempts to explain the laws of Moses and the teachings of the prophets, these Jewish theologians had lost sight of mercy, justice, and humility.

In Matthew 23:23–24, for instance, Jesus accused the religious leaders with these caustic words: "Woe to you, teachers of the law and Pharisees, you hypocrites! You give a tenth of your spices—mint, dill, and cummin. But you have neglected the more important matters of the law—justice, mercy, and faithfulness. You should have practiced the latter, without neglecting the former. You blind guides! You strain out a gnat but swallow a camel."

Jesus was born into a world of sorrow, religious hypocrisy, and political oppression. He did not come into the world to destroy the Mosaic Law or refute the words of the early prophets. He did come to attack hypocrisy. Yet that was only a secondary purpose. Foremost He was born to give His life for our sins and to free us from the curse of eternal death.

Jesus came to establish a radically new kingdom on earth. It was not to be a political kingdom, but a kingdom within each person's heart. It was to be a kingdom based upon love—a kind of love the world had never really known before.

Jesus Christ came into the world with a life-changing message for all who would listen. During His short-lived ministry, He went all over Israel healing the sick, casting out devils, raising the dead, and teaching the people about the kingdom of God.

He did not launch a political movement against Rome or agitate for the release of the slaves. He was concerned with changing the hearts of men and women, not their outward circumstances. He knew that once a radical change had taken place in their hearts, their outward circumstances would cease to have devastating effects on their lives. This "change of heart" is at the root of what Jesus taught and spoke regarding women in society.

WOMEN AND GOD'S WORD

To understand what Jesus taught about the relationships between men and women, consider the Genesis account of Creation.

Genesis 1 describes how God created the heavens, the earth, and all living creatures. On the sixth day He created man and woman, blessed them, and told them to have dominion over the earth. Adam and Eve were given joint authority to rule and subdue the planet. Significantly, when God created Adam, He realized it wasn't good for man to be alone. He knew that man lacked something and was incomplete.

So God put Adam to sleep and fashioned woman from one of his ribs. She was created *out of* and *for* man to make him complete. One author has written, ". . .She is man's complement, essential to the perfection of his being. Without her he is not man in the generic fullness of that term."[1] Woman was to be his helpmeet, companion, and friend. In the marriage relationship, she was literally fashioned to be Adam's "other half." Together, as a unity, they were given full authority over the world.

Unfortunately this close communion with God was dramatically altered when Eve ate the forbidden fruit and then gave it to Adam. Together they had sinned against God and were cut off from intimate fellowship with their loving Creator.

God punished the serpent for tempting them and Adam and Eve for sinning by yielding to the temptation. In Genesis 3, God tells the serpent, "Cursed are you above all the livestock and all the wild animals! You will crawl on your belly and you will eat dust all the days of your life" (v. 14).

To Eve, God said, "I will greatly increase your pains in childbearing; with pain you will give birth to children. Your desire will be for your husband, and he will rule over you" (v. 16).

To Adam, God said, "Cursed is the ground because of you; through painful toil you will eat of it all the days of your life. It will produce thorns and thistles for you, and you will eat the plants of the field. By the sweat of your brow you will eat your food until you return to the ground, since from it you were taken; for dust you are and to dust you will return" (vv. 17–19).

Because of the Fall, God altered the egalitarian relationship between man and woman, making them interdependent, but making man the head of the family.

In God's ideal marriage, there was to have been mutual admiration and respect; there was to have been love and cooperation. But when sin entered the world, the relationship between man and woman—between husband and wife—was distorted, corrupted by a natural desire to sin against each other.

When sin was let loose in the world, men and women fell victim to selfishness, exploitation, abuse, deceit, lust, and cruel domination. Women have suffered the most as a result of the Fall, primarily because of their lack of physical strength. They have been brutalized and oppressed for centuries in pagan cultures.

Women in Old Testament Times

In Exodus, Leviticus, Numbers, and Deuteronomy, God gave the Jewish people a variety of specific laws dealing with property rights, personal relationships, treatment of enemies, feast days, sacred rituals, and the treatment of wives and single women. There were even guidelines to protect women captured in battle. God gave the Israelites these laws because out of all nations, He had chosen them to be His special people. He wanted to demonstrate His love and glory through them if they were faithful to His commands. These laws were given to make Israel a holy, righteous, and strong nation, one that would remain pure and bring glory to God.

The holiness laws placed certain obligations on women. These laws dealt harshly with adulterers and sexual perverts and tended to create a strong family unit—the basic unit in any society.

In our "liberated" age—an age characterized by rebellion against all authority structures—it shocks our sensibilities to read Leviticus or Deuteronomy, with their stringent laws. These laws seem unfair, cruel, and often discriminatory to our way of thinking. But they were given to maintain the sanctity of marriage, safeguard the moral strength of the nation, and protect the Jewish people from intermarrying with heathens having idolatrous practices.

Women in particular benefited from these laws. For example, a widow was encouraged to marry her husband's brother or return to her father's house for shelter. Adultery and incest were punishable by death. Although women were generally held in high esteem in Jewish culture, they still had to submit to the God-ordained male authority structure.

Even Vern Bullough, who writes from a humanist perspective in *The Subordinate Sex—A History of Attitudes Toward Women,* observes, "In its positive aspects, the ancient Jewish attitude led to a high regard for home and children and a high ideal of family life. Though woman's domestic and maternal virtues were esteemed, she was subordinate and naturally inferior to man, and she labored under various religious and social disabilities."[2]

Another author has written, "Under the Hebrew system the position of woman was in marked contrast with her status in surrounding heathen nations. Her liberties were greater, her employments more varied and important, her social standing more respectful and commanding."[3]

JESUS AND THE LAW

The Lord never contradicted the writing of the Old Testament. In fact, in Matthew 5:17–18, Jesus tells a crowd, "Do not think that I have come to abolish the Law or Prophets; I have not come to abolish them but to fulfill them. I tell you the truth, until heaven and earth disappear, not the smallest letter, not the least stroke of a pen, will by any means disappear from the Law until everything is accomplished."

Jesus affirmed all that had been written in the Old Testament, but He did more than simply affirm the Scriptures. He spent much of His time clarifying many of the Old Testament moral laws. In Matthew 5:27–28, for example, He says, "You have heard that it was said, 'Do not commit adultery.' But I tell you that anyone who looks at a woman lustfully has already committed adultery with her in his heart."

Jesus was affirming the dignity and worth of women. It was just as wrong to *think* of fornicating with a woman as it was to actually commit the act. Women are to be treated as human beings, not as sex objects. It is *adultery* to lust after a woman. How it must grieve our Lord to see how women are degraded in pornographic movies, in striptease shows, on television, and in movies!

In Matthew 5:31–32 Jesus deals with the issue of divorce: "It has been said, 'Anyone who divorces his wife must give her a certificate of divorce.' But I tell you that anyone who divorces his wife, except for marital unfaithfulness, causes her to commit adultery, and anyone who marries a woman so divorced commits adultery." Here Jesus cries out against the devaluation of the marriage relationship. The Jewish scholars had become so hardened in their attitudes about divorce that a man could get rid of his wife for as simple an offense as burning the dinner. Jesus was declaring that the marriage vow was sacred—to be broken only because of adultery.

Once Jesus enraged the officials of the synagogue by healing a desperately ill woman on a Sabbath day. In Luke 13:10–17 we read that she had been afflicted by an evil spirit for eighteen years. She was bent over and couldn't straighten up. When Jesus saw her, He had compassion on her and said, "Woman, you are set free from your infirmity" (v. 12). He put His hands on her, and immediately she stood up and began praising God.

The official in the synagogue was angered at Jesus for healing anyone on the Sabbath. Instead of rejoicing that this woman had been released from eighteen years of agony, he told the crowd, "There are six days for work. So come and be healed on those days, not on the Sabbath" (v. 14). The Lord retorted, "You hypocrites! Doesn't each of you on the Sabbath untie his ox or donkey from the stall and lead it out to give it water? Then should not this woman, a daughter of Abraham, whom Satan has kept bound for eighteen long years, be set free on the Sabbath day from what bound her?" (vv. 15–16). His answer shamed the temple official.

On another occasion, a Pharisee had invited Jesus to his home for dinner. While Jesus was reclining at the table, a woman who had led a sinful life came into the Pharisee's house carrying an alabaster jar of perfume. When she had learned Jesus was in town, she wanted desperately to see Him. In Luke 7:36–50 we read how this penitent woman kneeled before Jesus, weeping uncontrollably, washed His feet with her tears and wiped them dry with her hair. She then anointed His head with perfume.

The Pharisee was insulted that Jesus would allow such behavior from a known harlot, and he said to himself, "If this man were a prophet, he would know who is touching him and what kind of woman she is— that she is a sinner" (v. 39).

Jesus knew the Pharisee's secret thoughts, of course, and told him a simple story to illustrate God's forgiveness. Two men, Jesus said, owed a creditor. One of them owed $500 while the other owed only $50. For some reason, the creditor decided to cancel the debts of both men. Jesus then asked the Pharisee, "Now which of them will love him more?" (v. 42). And the Pharisee answered, "I suppose the one who had the bigger debt canceled" (v. 43). That was the correct answer. Jesus told him that one who is forgiven much loves much. This woman had led a life of terrible sin, but she was showing her repentance by her actions. She was sorry for her sins and was seeking forgiveness. Jesus finally told her, "Your sins are forgiven. . . .Your faith has saved you; go in peace" (vv. 48–50).

Note that in these two illustrations, Jesus didn't rebuff the women. Both had serious needs—one physical, the other spiritual. In both cases Jesus showed them respect and met their needs.

Women in Jesus' Ministry

Women played an active role throughout Jesus' earthly ministry. Many prominent women helped support His ministry financially; others followed Him from city to city. They were there as He carried the cross to Calvary; they prayed for Him as He hung on the cross. And women were the first to learn of His resurrection.

Charles C. Ryrie has written in *The Role of Women in the Church*, "There can be no doubt that Jesus considered the two sexes equal. However, as regards spiritual activity, there was a difference between that of men and women. . . . It is significant that Jesus chose and sent out seventy men. It is significant that there was no woman chosen to be among the twelve disciples."[4]

It is in this matter of "equality" that we find so much controversy, both inside and outside the church. Within the church are "Christian" feminists who believe that much of what is taught about women in both the Old and New Testaments is simply a result of "cultural conditioning"—not God's specific instructions to His people. Feminist writers Letha Scanzoni and Nancy

Hardesty contend in their book, *All We're Meant to Be,* that God originally intended males and females to be "equal" not only in spiritual privilege, but in spiritual activity as well. They believe that when Paul spoke out against women teaching or having authority over men, he was dealing with a particular problem within a certain church. They believe women should be ordained and have the same leadership positions within the church as men.

In *Women and the Word of God,* Susan Foh takes issue with their position by noting, "Though Scanzoni and Hardesty support their conclusions with exegesis, their conclusions were decided beforehand. They and other biblical feminists approach the Bible with the preconceived idea that God neither could nor would make distinctions between women and men; God would not prohibit women from certain activity in the church on the basis of sex. This preconception depends on another more basic one: that God did not sovereignly speak His Word; God spoke through finite, culturally determined people, whose finiteness and culture discolored God's words. Man's words, commands, and theology are intermixed with God's."[5]

The cry for "equality" within the church and outside of it is dangerously deceptive. Scanzoni and Hardesty, for instance, claim that "To argue that women are equal in creation, but subordinate in function, is no more defensible than 'separate but equal schools' for the races."[6] The truth is, however, that men and women *are* radically different, not only physically, but in their thought processes as well. They can in no sense ever be "equal" in all areas of endeavor.

In the marriage relationship especially, there is clear teaching from the Word of God that the husband is the head of the family. The wife, of course, is supposed to have a say in how the family functions, but in no sense is she to be an "equal" in leadership. Nor does it mean she is "inferior" simply because she is second in command in the home. One writer has observed, "Priority of creation may indicate headship, but not, as theologians have so uniformly affirmed, superiority. Dependence indicates difference of function, not inferiority. Human values are estimated in terms of the mean and spiritual."[7]

To be a helper or a subordinate to someone does not mean to be inferior to that person. In marriage, both husband and wife have vitally important roles to fulfill. One job is not more important than the other. Both are essential if the family is to prosper. Every organization must have a leader. We cannot have a smooth-running company without someone to head it and give it direction.

Trying to explain away the clear teachings of Scripture dealing with husband-and-wife relationships is rebelling against what God has ordained from the creation of the world. True, men have often abused their right to headship within the family. In *What's a Woman to Do ... In the Church?* David R. Nicholas remarked, "Let's face it, some Christian husbands have the idea that their 'headship' in the home constitutes a license to lord it over their wives like little Caesars. They act as though their wives are incidental and of secondary importance in their lives. A wife is given little opportunity to realize the potential God has given her, and she ends up feeling like a professional 'house drudge,' and a modern-day slave."[8]

A husband who acts this way is sinning against the Lord and his wife, as we'll see in the next section.

THE APOSTLE PAUL AND WOMEN

Paul has been the target of much abuse from feminists and humanists. They see him as a male chauvinist, a misogynist who wanted to keep women in silence, ignorance, and bondage. One radical feminist has written, "Androcentric tendencies in Western culture, rooted also in the profound misogynism of the Greeks, are reflected in the New Testament as well, which in turn has served as the basis for their perpetuation throughout Christendom. The most strikingly antifeminine passages are in the Pauline texts. . . . It seemed important to him that women should not have a predominant place in Christian assemblies, that they should not 'speak' in public or unveil their heads."[9]

When I read Paul's epistles, I see an entirely different man. Before Paul experienced his dramatic conversion to Christ on the road to Damascus, he was known as Saul of Tarsus, a zealous Pharisee who was using all his energies to persecute the young Christian church. He had been educated under Gamaliel, the most famous Jewish theologian of the time, and had been standing nearby when Stephen, the first Christian martyr, was stoned to death. Yet when the Lord spoke to him from heaven, he willingly obeyed.

Paul contributed more to the growth of the Christian church than any of the other apostles. God had called him to take the Good News of Jesus Christ to the Gentile nations. He suffered persecution—beatings, jail sentences, shipwrecks, and more—all because he was being obedient to God's call.

In his letters to the churches, Paul deals with doctrine and personal relationships—especially between husbands and wives. For example, writing to the Ephesians, he says, "Submit to one another out of reverence for Christ. Wives, submit to your husbands as to the Lord. For the husband is the head of the wife as Christ is the head of the church, his body, of which he is the Savior. Now as the church submits to Christ, so also wives should submit to their husbands in everything. Husbands, love your wives, just as Christ loved the church and gave himself up for her to make her holy, cleansing her by the washing with water through the word, and to present her to himself as a radiant church, without stain or wrinkle or any other blemish, but holy and blameless" (Eph. 5:21–28).

Paul also told husbands that they were to love their wives as they loved their own bodies! He writes, "The husband should fulfill his marital duty to his wife, and likewise the wife to her husband. In the same way, the husband's body does not belong to him alone but also to his wife" (1 Cor. 7:3–4).

In all these writings Paul is imposing obligations upon *both* the wife and husband to love, respect, and submit to each other. Yet the husband is still the head of the family, just as Christ is to be the head and ruler over the husband. There is simply no place in a Christian marriage for an overbearing, ruthless husband who rules as a dictator. If he loves his wife as Christ loved the church, he will be willing to lose his own life for her if necessary. Both Paul and Jesus Christ taught a *self*-sacrificing love between marriage partners.

Women in the Church

Because of the Fall, men and women have different roles to play within the church as within marriage. In 1 Timothy 2:8–14, Paul says, "I want men everywhere to lift up holy hands in prayer, without anger or disputing. I also want women to dress modestly, with decency and propriety, not with braided hair or gold or pearls or expensive clothes, but with good deeds, appropriate for women who profess to worship God. A woman should learn in quietness and full submission. I do not permit a woman to teach or to have authority over a man; she must be silent. For Adam was formed first, then Eve. And Adam was not the one deceived; it was the woman who was deceived and became a sinner."

This passage of Scripture has been the subject of endless debate in the church and has been used by feminists and humanists to show how undemocratic and authoritarian the Christian church is. I believe it means precisely what it says: Women are not to teach or have positions of authority over men in the church. Men have authority in the church because they represent Christ (Eph. 5:23).

However, this does not mean that women have *no* place in the church. In the first-century church, women were very active in works of mercy, charity, and good deeds. Very often prominent women opened their homes to the apostles on their travels, and home churches were often started by women. Lydia, for example, was the first convert to Christianity in Europe, and she offered her home as a meeting place (Acts 16).

Priscilla and Aquila were apparently an active husband-and-wife team in the early church, expounding on the Word of God to such zealous preachers as Apollos (Acts 18:14–15)).

In Romans 16, Paul sends his love and greetings to several women who were actively involved in spreading the Good News of Jesus Christ. He says, "I commend to you our sister Phoebe, a servant of the church in Cenchrea. I ask you to receive her in the Lord in a way worthy of the saints and give her any help she may need from you, for she has been a great help to many people, including me. Greet Priscilla and Aquila, my fellow workers in Christ Jesus. They risked their lives for me. Not only I but all the churches of the Gentiles are grateful to them. Greet also the church that meets at their house" (vv. 1–5). And in Colossians 4:15 he says, "Give my greetings to the brothers in Laodicea, and to Nympha and the church in her house."

Paul appreciated the dedication of women to the work of the Lord. He was not a misogynist.

Women have many areas of ministry to fulfill within the church. By being sensitive to the leading of the Spirit, women will find out how much freedom they do have. They can serve as deacons, as Phoebe did in the first-century church; they can participate in visitation programs, help prepare Communion, promote Christian education, help with mission programs, assist in personal evangelism, and write for Christian publications.

Unfortunately women have not always been motivated or encouraged to use their talents within the church. Stuart Briscoe writes in *Moody Monthly* that ". . .the greatest wasted resource in the church is woman-power." He says the church has been remiss in not allowing women more freedom in the exercise of their gifts, and he concludes, "I need to ensure that the women in my life have every encouragement from me to be what He called and gifted them to be. A major part of my life must be spent as a man caring for, nurturing, encouraging and developing gifted women, because they aren't the only ones who will give account for their stewardship. As a man in a male-oriented church, I may one day be asked about *their* gifts, too. I would like to be able to say I did considerably more than burying. A talent is a terrible thing to waste."[10]

THE CHURCH FATHERS AND GOD'S WORD

Tragically, the teachings of Jesus, Paul, and the other apostles regarding male-female relationships became distorted before the last apostle died.

In *The Women and the Liberator,* William P. Barker writes, "The church has never caught up with Jesus. In spite of an auspicious start, where its corporate life reflected the truth that 'there is neither male nor female; we are all one in Christ Jesus.' By the third century A.D., the church fell into its own kind of double standard."[11]

Barker believes that the teachings of the monastics led to a degraded view of women in the church. As a result of the monastic writers' faulty thinking and bad theology, they ". . .stained all subsequent theology and the church has yet to rinse it out."[12]

The pagan philosophy of Gnosticism subtly invaded the Christian church, and, as an anti-Christian belief system, has done immense damage to the cause of Christ and to a clear, scriptural view of women's rights and responsibilities in church and society. One writer observed that Gnosticism ". . .endeavored to introduce into Christianity a so-called higher knowledge, which was grounded partly on the philosophic creed in which Greeks and Romans had taken refuge consequent on the gradual decay and breaking-up of their own religions, partly . . . on the philosophies of Plato and of Philo, and still more on the philosophies and theosophies and religions of the East, especially those of Persia and of India."[13]

One of the main beliefs in Gnosticism was the concept that matter is evil and is the source from which all evil has come. Another concept is that Jesus Christ is not truly human because He could not possibly have allowed Himself to be tainted by living in a material body.

From these ideas, the Gnostics went further and believed that ". . .sin is inherent in the material substance of the body; therefore, the only way by which perfection can be reached is to punish the body by asceticism, so that through the infliction of pain and the mortification of the flesh the region of pure spirit may be reached, and thus man may be etherealized and become like God."[14]

One of the earliest Gnostics was Tatian, who led a group calling themselves the Encratites or the "self-controlled." They abstained from sexual intercourse, intoxicating beverages, and meat. They believed that marriage would corrupt the body and prevent one from becoming holy. Sexual desire was considered a great sin; and because it was woman who created this sexual desire, she was abhorred. She was viewed with suspicion and fear—an evil material being capable of keeping a man from communing with "God."

Marcion was another Gnostic philosopher whose ideas corrupted the simplicity of the gospel and of Jesus' respect for women. Marcion did not believe in the virgin birth of Jesus and refused to accept the reality of Jesus' death on the cross. One author has written of Marcion, "He insisted on the importance of complete abstinence from sexual intercourse; carnal lusts were bad in themselves, and the normal consequence of sexual desires was also bad. . . ."[15] The Marcionites refused to baptize married couples because they had engaged in sexual intercourse.

During the first and second centuries the Gnostics and other self-proclaimed theologians began to warp and corrupt the Word of God. Charles C. Ryrie has written, "There is a definite beginning of an ascetic strain in Christian teaching during this period. Along with this, as one would naturally expect, came a tendency on the part of some to prefer celibacy; but often celibacy is presented merely as an alternative, and not in preference, to marriage."[16]

There evolved two diverse strains of religious thought during these early centuries. One group of theologians exalted virgin women while others began to construct rigid theories about the supposed inferiority of women, of their decadence, and of the need to keep them in subjection because they aroused sexual desire in men.

The monks, for example, were constantly warring against their natural God-given desires, falsely believing that sexual desire was sinful. Their low view of women is characterized by the statement of the fourth-century church father John Chrysostom, who writes, "Woman is a necessary evil, a national temptation, a desirable calamity, a domestic peril, a deadly fascination, and a painted evil."[17]

This fourth-century thinking has not been completely eradicated. In fact, there are men today who consider women to be inferior and slander them. Sadly, some of these are even ministers of the gospel who make belittling and humiliating comments from their pulpits. This results in a subtle message to the men—especially young men in the congregation—that women are not to be as highly regarded as men.

SUMMARY

When God created male and female, He sought close fellowship with both. Sin brought a tragic separation in that relationship. Only through the sacrificial death of Jesus Christ was this special communion reestablished.

When Jesus preached, He sought to demonstrate to the Jewish world that men and women are equal before God, but He did nothing to change the headship role of the husband in marriage. Later Paul wrote in the epistles, that husbands were obligated to love their wives with the same kind of caring love that Jesus had shown for His church—a willingness to give up His life for it. That kind of obligation puts a serious burden on the shoulders of a man to carry out his responsibilities within the family. It must be done in love, respect, and compassion.

Many of the church fathers, though well-intentioned, may have distorted the meaning of the Scriptures. The Gnostic heresy also contributed to a low view of women throughout history. These prejudices have been passed down from generation to generation. This low view of women has prevented the Christian church from fully benefiting from the many talents of women, talents that could have been used to bring glory to God. This neglect of women may be partially responsible for the national turmoil and restlessness regarding women.

NOTES

[1] "Women," *International Standard Bible Encyclopedia*, vol. 5 (Grand Rapids: Eerdmans, 1960), 3100.

[2] Vern L. Bullough, *The Subordinate Sex—A History of Attitudes Toward Women* (Urbana, Ill.: Univ. of Illinois Press, 1973), 49.

[3] "Women," *ISBE*, 3100.

[4] Charles C. Ryrie, *The Role of Women in the Church* (Chicago: Moody Press, 1958), 28–29.

[5] Susan T. Foh, *Women and the Word of God—A Response to Biblical Feminism* (Phillipsburg, Pa.: Presbyterian and Reformed, 1980), 48.

[6] Nancy Hardesty and Letha Scanzoni, *All We're Meant to Be* (Waco, Tex.: Word Books, 1975), 205.

[7] "Women," *ISBE*, 3100.

[8] David R. Nicholas, *What's a Woman to Do . . . In the Church?* (Scottsdale, Ariz.: Good Life Publications, 1979), 121.

[9] Philip P. Wiener, ed., *Dictionary of the History of Ideas* (New York: Scribner's, 1973), 524.

[10] Stuart Briscoe, "The Biblical Woman: We've Buried Treasure," *Moody Monthly* (February 1983): 6.

[11] William P. Barker, *The Women and the Liberator* (Old Tappan, N.J.: Fleming H. Revell, 1972), 11.

[12] Ibid.

[13] "Gnosticism," *ISBE*, vol. 2, 1240.

[14] Ibid., 1242.

[15] T. A. Burkill, *The Evolution of Christian Thought* (Ithaca, N.Y.: Cornell Univ. Press, 1977), 42–43.

[16] Ryrie, *The Role of Women*, 102.

[17] Briscoe, "The Biblical Woman," 6.

3.

Spreading Turmoil
in Early America

The American feminists of the nineteenth century were a powerful force in our society. Though always small in number, these zealous women took leadership roles in the antislavery movement of the middle 1800s. They rallied alongside their male abolitionist counterparts in laboring for an end to the institution of slavery. They were also concerned about gaining "freedom" for themselves, but it was a freedom of a different kind.

The feminist movement has several root causes. Three of the most obvious are the Industrial Revolution, the French Revolution, and parental or marital problems.

CHILD ABUSE AND NEGLECT

As I studied the lives of many early feminists, I found that the majority of them were either cruelly treated by their mothers or fathers, or they simply couldn't cope with their rigid, humorless religious upbringings. In either case these feminists saw themselves as victims of a patriarchal society that based its "male domination" upon the Scriptures. Thus they rejected not only their fathers, but also basic social foundations because they felt it had brought them only misery, emotional turmoil, and oppression. In a very real sense, uncaring men—whether as fathers or husbands, spawned the radical feminist revolution. I wonder how many times a father's misinterpretation of the Scriptures or undue harshness in applying scriptural principles drove his daughter to despair and finally to a total rejection of Christ.

These women who couldn't find the warmth, care, and love they desperately needed from their fathers or their husbands became embittered revolutionaries, dedicated to overthrowing the marriage relationship and other social institutions. It is little wonder that these women could not relate to a loving heavenly Father when they had broken relationships with their earthly fathers.

CHANGES IN WORK

The Industrial Revolution brought drastic social changes that directly affected the relationships between husbands, wives, and children. With the invention of the steam engine, our agricultural society was rapidly transformed into an industrial nation. The nature of work changed as a result. When we were an agrarian society, families worked together either on farms or in family businesses. A husband, wife, and children were all intimately involved with one another. The father was in charge of the family, but there was a closeness, a bonding between all members of the family that seldom exists anymore.

With the increase in corporate businesses and factory work, the father went off to work, the children went off to school, and the mother stayed at home to cook, iron, and clean. In those simpler times before industrialization, every family member was an economic asset, contributing to the livelihood of the family. The home was the center of economic, social, and spiritual activity. Today it has increasingly become merely a place where people eat and sleep.

The Industrial Revolution was both a blessing and a curse to many middle-class women. Although it gave them more freedom from household chores, it left a vacuum within them that needed to be filled by something—something they felt was "socially useful." The feminist movement was led, according to one historian, by educated, middle-class women who, "...robbed of any useful function in the home and unable to find meaningful and well-paying jobs outside of it, felt a great deal of frustration."[1]

Carl Wilson writes in *Our Dance Has Turned to Death*, "While man has essentially built a tower to reach heaven, he has unwittingly locked his housewife counterpart into a closet, giving her little to do."[2] To cope with growing feelings of uselessness, many of these women became involved in forming women's clubs and social reform movements. They organized temperance unions, outreaches for prostitutes, antislavery organizations, and crusaded against child labor abuses. Unfortunately, others became leaders in radical feminist causes.

The industrialization of our country tended to separate man's work from woman's work. The man went off to the office and received a paycheck for his productivity; the woman stayed home and did not receive a paycheck. In the eyes of many radical feminists, this arrangement was nothing short of slavery. To them, the only way women could truly be free was to cut themselves loose from the bonds of marriage and find work outside the home.

Ferdinand Lundberg and Marynia Farnham write, "The destruction of the traditional home has been emotionally hazardous to men, women and children. But it has affected no one more destructively than women, and is the root cause of modern women's restlessness and discontent, shown in so many ways."[3]

THE HUMANIST REVOLUTION

The French Revolution was another catalyst in the rise of the feminist movement in America. The writings of radical anarchists and pre-Marx "communists" were adopted by American feminists in their efforts to re-structure the "patriarchal" and "capitalist" society.

According to historian James H. Billington, women played a leading role in revolutionary activities in Europe during this period. During the 1840s, for example, the French feminist-writer George Sand was busy promoting her brand of socialism through her novels. Billington writes, "The example of George Sand helped implant within Russia the revolutionary consciousness that prepared the way for 1905 and 1917. The two greatest writers who participated in pioneering socialist circles of the 1840s in Russia, [Feodor] Dostoevsky and [Mikhail Evgratovich] Saltykov, both considered Sand a leading force in activating their social consciousness and one of the supreme personalities of the century."[4]

Sand, who was born Amandine Aurore Lucie Dupin, took a man's name and wore men's clothing. She once wrote, "I continue to believe that marriage is one of the most hateful of institutions. I have no doubt whatever that when the human race has advanced further toward rationality and the love of justice, marriage will be abolished. A human and not less sacred union would then replace it, and the existence of the children would be not less cared for and secured, without therefore binding in eternal fetters the freedom of the parents."[5]

A Vindication of the Rights of Woman

Mary Wollenstonecraft is considered by many feminists to be the "founding mother" of the nineteenth-century feminist movement, just as today Betty Friedan is considered the "founding mother" of the late twentieth-century movement. In 1792 Mary published her major work, *A Vindication of the Rights of Woman*. One feminist author has called this book ". . .the most important of a number of feminist works published in the latter part of the eighteenth century."[6]

Vindication is like a feminist Magna Carta. It is a foundational document that has been added to, amended, and expanded upon by radical feminists for two centuries. In their book *Modern Woman—The Lost Sex*, authors Lundberg and Farnham detail the tragic life of Mary Wollenstonecraft. They observe that her life ". . .reads like a psychiatric case history. So, for that matter, do the lives of many later feminists."[7]

Mary hated men and not without good reason. She was born in 1759, second of six children. Her father was a vulgar drunkard who regularly beat his wife and terrorized the children. Because of her father's irresponsibility, the family was always on the move, existing as drifters, with no reason to live.

Her sad home life eventually destroyed her. She was never able to have normal, healthy relationships with men although she literally threw herself at them. She desperately needed to be loved and accepted, but the psychological damage done to her during childhood was too much for her ever to overcome. In Paris in 1792 she met Capt. Gilbert Imlay, an American officer who served under George Washington. He never really cared about her, but got her pregnant and then deserted her.

Mary tried to poison herself at one point, then threw herself into the Thames River in a second suicide attempt. When she met William Godwin, an anarchist, he too got her pregnant. They finally did marry, but she died following complications after giving birth to Mary Godwin.

From birth to death, Mary Wollenstonecraft was a tortured woman—a woman who had been deprived of a loving home environment where she could have grown into a happy, well-adjusted adult. Even after her death, her children were seemingly driven to self-destruction. Her oldest daughter, Fanny Imlay, committed suicide at nineteen. Her second daughter, Mary, began having an affair with Percy Shelley when Shelley was already married to Harriet Westbrook. The love affair drove Shelley's wife to suicide.[8]

Looking at Mary Wollenstonecraft's life, I can only feel pity. She was a victim of the sin in her father's life. As a result, she grew up to be a neurotic—a man-hater who sought vengeance by striking out at society. Other leaders of the feminist movement have had similarly flawed childhoods. Lundberg and Farnham write, "This ideology ... we regard as an expression of emotional sickness, of neurosis. Feminism, despite the external validity of its political program and most (not all) of its social program, was at its core a deep illness."[9]

THE GOALS OF NINETEENTH-CENTURY FEMINISTS

According to feminist writer Miriam Schnier, the feminists of the late 1700s and 1800s had identified ". . .marriage as a primary instrument of women's oppression. . . . Another theme of central importance to the old as well as the new feminism is the economic dependence of women."[10] Still another goal was the "selfhood" of women. Schnier says, "The dominant male society suppresses woman's individuality, inhibits her intelligence and talent, and forces her to assume standards of appearance and personality that coincide with the masculine ideal of how a woman should behave and look."[11]

The same themes are being promoted in feminist writings today: destruction of the family; advocacy of women in the work force to assure "equality" with men, and the glorification of hedonistic selfishness—"doing your own thing" without any regard for how your actions might hurt others. For more than two centuries this feminist agenda has not changed. The personages are different, but the goals remain the same.

Two Feminist Leaders

Elizabeth Cady Stanton and Lucy Stone, among others, took a lead in the feminist movement of the 1800s. Elizabeth Stanton rejected her stern Presbyterian upbringing and became a liberal Quaker as she became more closely involved in the antislavery movement. For several years she carried on an affair with her sister's husband, but in 1840 married Henry Brewster Stanton, an abolitionist. Immediately after the ceremony, they sailed for London to attend the World Anti-Slavery Convention.

Elizabeth's radical leanings were further enflamed when she and her husband moved to Boston. There she met Frederick Douglass, Lydia Maria Child, John Greenleaf Whittier, and other liberal freethinkers.

It was Elizabeth who helped to organize the famous First Women's Rights Convention at Seneca Falls, New York, in 1848. She also drafted the "Declaration of Sentiments" based on the phrasing of the Declaration of Independence. In the "Declaration" she enumerated the complaints "women" had against "men" and then offered several resolutions.

Elizabeth was a tireless worker for the feminist cause. Her rebellious nature is evident in a remark she once made: "It is a settled maxim with me, that the existing public sentiment on any subject is wrong."[12] Her opinion of religion was not much different. In an article published in *North American Review* in 1888, she observed that women are ". . .not indebted to any form of religion for one step of progress, nor one new liberty; on the contrary, it has been through the perversion of her religious sentiments that she has been so long held in a condition of slavery."[13] She was so convinced that the Bible was biased against women that she wrote *The Woman's Bible*, reinterpreting the Scriptures to fit her own viewpoint.

Lucy Stone was another prominent activist. She too was convinced of the inaccuracy of the Bible and studied Greek and Hebrew to prove the male biases of Scripture. After graduating from Oberlin College, she worked as a lecturer in the American Anti-Slavery Society.

Early in life Lucy had decided against marriage, but eventually at age thirty-seven she married Henry Blackwell. However, she refused to use his name. In 1866 she helped organize the American Equal Rights Association, pressing for Negro and woman suffrage. In 1872 she assumed editorial responsibility for the weekly feminist newspaper *Woman's Journal*.[14]

Spiritualism, Communism, and Free Love

Victoria Woodhull and her sister Tennessee Claflin were two of the most radical feminists of the era. Their extreme stands on every social issue make Lucy Stone and Elizabeth Stanton look like devout Christians. One author described Woodhull in this manner: "Victoria Woodhull's father, Ruben Buckman Claflin, was a confirmed psychopath; her mother Roxanna was a superstitious mystic who experienced visions. Not surprisingly, Victoria, born in 1838, became a psychopathic mystic."[15]

Victoria was married at the age of fifteen to Canning Woodhull, a man who turned out to be an alcoholic lecher. Their marriage was over quickly. She and her sister traveled with her father and mother selling cancer cures and promoting Tennessee's psychic abilities.

In 1868 Victoria and Tennessee met Commodore Vanderbilt, and Tennessee became his mistress. By 1869, with the generous help of Vanderbilt, the two sisters became the first women to become Wall Street brokers. Jean Blashfield says of this, "Seances held by Victoria, magic magnetic treatments, and Tennessee in his bed made the Commodore quite receptive when Victoria suggested that he might like to back them in their new enterprise. Their firm immediately prospered, clearing a profit of two-thirds of a million dollars in the first three years."[16]

Vanderbilt was also the chief financial backer of their radical feminist newspaper, *Woodhull and Claflin's Weekly*. Their newspaper was filled with lurid articles on venereal disease, eugenics, abortion, free love, spiritualism, working-woman issues, and socialism. Their newspaper holds the distinction of being the first in America to publish the *Communist Manifesto.*

Victoria ran for the presidency of the United States in 1872, but was in jail at the time, having been arrested for publishing an obscene article. She was elected president of the American Association of Spiritualists and in 1873 spoke at their annual convention in Chicago. During that speech she said, "The wife who submits to sexual intercourse against her wishes or desires, virtually commits suicide; while the husband who compels it, commits murder, and ought just as much to be punished for it, as though he strangled her to death for refusing him."[17]

Communism and Feminism

Marxist thought has been intimately involved in the feminist movement. In the book *Feminism: The Essential Historical Writings,* Miriam Schnier cites portions of Friedrich Engel's writings that purport to explain the origin of families and the "patriarchal" system. Engel's atheistic view of family life and his call for the destruction of the capitalist system have become the foundation of many feminist writings. In his essay, "The Origin of the Family, Private Property, and the State," Engel says that women are treated as property or as wage slaves within the family system. The wife, he states, is not much better than a prostitute ". . .who only differs from the ordinary courtesan in that she does not let out her body on piece-work as a wage-worker, but sells it once and for all into slavery."[18]

In the *Communist Manifesto* we read, "Abolition of the family! Even the most radical flare up at this infamous proposal of the Communists. On what foundation is the present family, the bourgeois family, based? On capital, on private gain. In its completely developed form this family exists only among the bourgeoisie. But this state of things finds its complement in the practical absence of the family among proletarians and in public prostitution."[19]

The Communists believe that women have been oppressed in capitalist countries as wage-slaves. They will only be liberated when they are able to go out into the work world and earn the same wages as men. To the Communists, the traditional family must be destroyed because they view it as the most basic unit of a capitalist system. They also believe that women must be radicalized if the Communist revolution is to succeed.

Stalin once wrote, "Working women—workers and peasants—are the greatest reserve of the working class. This reserve constitutes a good half of the population. The fate of the proletarian movement, the victory or defeat of the proletarian revolution, the victory or defeat of proletarian power depends on whether or not the reserve of women will be for or against the working class."[20]

THE COMMON THREADS

Several common threads of thought seem to keep appearing in feminist writings. These viewpoints are foundational to radical feminist beliefs: (1) hatred of God and authority figures; (2) rebellion based on selfishness; (3) belief in either anarchy or totalitarian communism; (4) advocacy of totally unrestrained behavior, abortion on demand, easy divorce; (5) disdain for family life and children; and (6) a commitment to atheism or spiritualism.

There is no way a philosophy based on hatred, anger, and rebellion can bring forth any positive results in our society. One of the greatest mistakes these early nineteenth-century feminists made was in seeking *self-fulfillment* instead of seeking to help others. But the philosophy of the world is diametrically opposed to the wisdom of God. The Word of God implies that only in giving do we receive; only in dying to ourselves do we find true peace and happiness. These statements seem paradoxical, but they are true. Only a person who has the indwelling Holy Spirit can understand the profound truths of the Bible. These troubled, neurotic women who rejected Jesus Christ had turned away from the only person who could have given them the kind of all-encompassing love they lacked. But they were too busy hating men to seek the Lord.

Feminism is more than an illness; it is a philosophy of death. At its core in modern times there is a stridently antilife motivation. Radical feminists are self-destructive and are trying to bring about the death of an entire civilization as well. What will be the ultimate destination of a society that adopts lesbianism, homosexuality, euthanasia, suicide, and abortion as positive elements? Death and more death. May God deliver us from those women who are determined to kill not only their own maternal instincts, but also unborn babies, the deformed, and the aged.

NOTES

[1] Emma Nyun-Han, "The American Women's Rights Movements: A Historical Overview," *The Westmont College Magazine* (February 1981), 13.

[2] Carl W. Wilson, *Our Dance Has Turned to Death* (Wheaton, Ill.: Tyndale House, 1981), 63.

[3] Ferdinand Lundberg and Marynia F. Farnham, *Modern Woman — The Lost Sex* (New York: Harper Brothers, 1947), 117.

[4] James H. Billington, *Fire in the Minds of Men* (New York: Basic Books, 1980), 402.

[5] Lundberg and Farnham, *Modern Woman—The Lost Sex*, 192.

[6] Miriam Schnier, ed., *Feminism: The Essential Historical Writings* (New York: Vintage Books, 1972), 5.

[7] Lundberg and Farnham, *Modern Woman—The Lost Sex*, 144.

[8] Ibid., 158.

[9] Ibid., 143.

[10] Schnier, *Feminism: The Essential Historical Writings*, xv.

[11] Ibid., xvi.

[12] Edward T. James, ed., *Notable American Women, 1607–1950* (Cambridge, Mass.: Belknap Press, Harvard Univ. Press, 1971), 344.

[13] Mary Ann B. Oakley, *Elizabeth Cady Stanton* (Old Westbury, N.Y.: Feminist Press, 1972), 112.

[14] James, *Notable American Women, 1607–1950*, 389.

[15] Bernard I. Murstein, *Love, Sex, and Marriage Through the Ages* (New York: Springer, 1974), 368.

[16] Jean F. Blashfield, *Hellraisers, Heroines, and Holy Women* (New York: St. Martin's, 1981), 23.

[17] Schnier, *Feminism: The Essential Historical Writings*, 153.

[18] Ibid., 197.

[19] Karl Marx et al., *The Essential Left* (New York: Barnes & Noble, 1963), 31.

[20] *The Woman Question: Selected Writings of Marx, Engels, Lenin, Stalin* (New York: International Publishers, 1951), 44.

4.

The World's Treatment of Women

A few years ago, when my husband Tim was pastoring a church, we were given a sabbatical leave to travel through Europe, Asia, and the Middle East. During the year we visited more than forty countries and talked with hundreds of pastors and laymen.

That trip—and others since then—gave us a better understanding of how women are treated in other nations. We found that only in countries where Christianity has been practiced have women had any measure of status, honor, or freedom in their society.

In nations where Jesus Christ has not been honored, women have been treated as little more than workhorses or servants. We lived for three weeks with a typical family in India. The father was a rigid patriarch, ruling over his wife and children. I quickly learned that in Indian culture, women are not to speak unless spoken to. Because I was from another culture, the Indian men relaxed some of their restrictions, and I was allowed to eat with them. But the Indian women had to stay in the kitchen until the men were finished eating; then they were allowed to eat. The traditional role for women in India is to serve men and be their sexual companions.

The classical writings of Hinduism teach that "no woman of any caste could gain salvation, except in a future life, when she had been reborn as a man."[1] The Hindu religion fosters the belief that being born a woman is the result of "bad karma." Men feel that the only way a woman can really be worth anything is when she is finally reincarnated as a man.

There was a time in India when it was customary for a widow to climb on the funeral pyre of her deceased husband to join him in the next life. She allowed herself to burn to death to show him respect. When the British ruled India, they prohibited this terrible practice. Yet today the status of women in India is not much improved.

WOMEN IN THE WORLD

We women in America often take our freedoms for granted. When "liberated" women talk about how oppressed we are, they're often reacting out of ignorance of the truth. Women in America enjoy more freedoms and opportunities than women anywhere else in the world.

World Vision International, a Christian relief organization that works in underdeveloped nations, has gathered startling statistics about women. For example, women are the sole providers for their families in nearly half of the developing countries. Nearly 75 percent of the women in the world are illiterate. In the Third World nations two out of three pregnant women are anemic. The birth of a boy in most of these nations is greeted with joy and singing; a baby girl is greeted with silence and disappointment. A boy is considered more important to the economic survival of the family and is nursed and cared for much longer than a baby girl. As a result, girls are more likely to be malnourished and brain damaged.[2]

Religion and Women

In Muslim and Hindu nations women are restricted to certain roles based on religious teachings. The religious laws in Bangladesh, for example, stress not just the subordination of women but also their inferiority. One legal study discloses that a woman "should do nothing independently even in her own house. In childhood subject to her father, in youth to her husband, and when her husband is dead to her sons. She should never enjoy independence."[3]

A Muslim man often has such strict control over his wife that she cannot even fast without her husband's permission. One author notes, "A woman's failure to obtain such permission resulted in her being shot and killed as late as 1977."[4]

In a Muslim nation such as Egypt, middle- and upper-class women are secluded in their homes and must wear veils. This practice is known as *purdah,* which means "curtain." It is based on the Muslim belief that women are weak and irresponsible and will tempt men to commit sexual immorality. Family honor is based on the virtue of its female members. To ensure that no man will be tempted to sexual sin, women are kept in their homes and veiled.[5]

Marriage and motherhood, however, are given high status in Egyptian society. The woman has almost complete authority in running her household, but that's the only role she is allowed.

I do not believe that our Lord intended women to be secluded in their homes and restricted to childbearing and household chores. Keeping the home should be a high priority for a woman, but there is nothing in the Bible that justifies the kind of treatment women receive in Muslim and Hindu nations. Jesus gave women a place of honor in the world. Non-Christian religions put women in an inferior position.

Women in Africa

Pagan religions, witchcraft, and the traditions of men have kept women in bondage in African countries. Fewer than one-third of the children attending primary schools in Africa are girls. Without an education these girls are economic liabilities to their families, so they are forced to marry when they're eleven or twelve or thirteen years old.[6] They have babies too soon and many die in childbirth. These are children giving birth to children. These young girls live out their lives having children, barely eking out a living in countries lacking many resources for food production.

The life of most African women is bleak. A World Vision team in Ethiopia several years ago discovered that among the women surveyed, 75 percent spent three hours on a single journey to collect water for their families. In some villages in East Africa, women leave at dawn and don't return until afternoon in their search for water.[7]

One of the most appalling practices against women in Africa is genital mutilation. Women are subjected to painful clitoridectomy, where the clitoris is cut off; or infibulation, where the vagina is sewn nearly shut. The clitoris is removed in the belief that it will purify her and make her more completely a woman.[8] These forms of genital mutilation are practiced in Kenya, Tanzania, Ethiopia, Sudan, Uganda, Zaire, Chad, Nigeria, Dahomey, Sierra Leone, and elsewhere.

Some feminist writers look on life in primitive societies as the ultimate in women's liberation. One writer claims that the women in Sierra Leone have self-esteem and social respect. They gain a sense of "sisterhood" through the practice of clitoridectomy. Developing close ties "is one purpose of clitoridectomy, the practice of excising the initiate's clitoris. This painful process is performed amid strong group songs and dances."[9]

Women in Mexico

The status of women in Mexico is probably typical of the way they're treated in other Latin American nations. Mexican women are respected as wives and mothers, but the husband often holds a double standard. He wants his wife to display the qualities of purity, patience, humility, and sacrifice, but he is free to do whatever he likes. It's not uncommon for him to have a mistress. One author writes, "Men put women on a pedestal and simultaneously relegate them to a life of suffering by being inattentive and unfaithful."[10]

There is no seclusion of women in Mexican society. They're expected to work in the fields and keep care of the house and children as well. And a woman does gain status within the family. If she cannot depend on her husband to meet her emotional needs, she can rely on her relatives in the extended family.

WOMEN AND COMMUNISM

This chapter provides only a sketchy overview of how women are and have been treated in other nations. My point is that women *have* been mistreated, oppressed, and deprived of their rights by men throughout the history of the world.

Yet some feminist writers seem to believe that women are "free" only when they work in the fields with men or when they can deposit their children in day-care centers and pursue their own fancies. The feminist viewpoint emphasizes the worth of a woman in economic terms. To the committed feminist, no woman is worth anything unless she's out in the world earning a paycheck. Some feminists believe that "equality" with men means having the dubious "right" to fight wars, climb telephone poles, weld, pour concrete, or unload cargo ships.

Other feminists mouth Marxist slogans taken from the writings of Karl Marx, Friedrich Engels, and others. During our travels in Europe, Tim and I visited Russia to see firsthand how the people lived. I vividly remember standing by the Kremlin Wall watching a work crew repair broken places in the wall. Backed up against the wall was a huge dump truck. Standing in this truck was an elderly woman with stooped shoulders, her face lined with years of suffering.

This woman's job was to chip away at the huge chunks of broken concrete and guide them into the truck. Tim and I watched this poor, miserable woman for perhaps twenty minutes. We realized that she was doomed to work at this job until the day she died. There would be no rest for her—just a tragic existence, breaking rock day after day. She was sharing in the "equality" of sexes guaranteed by the Communists.

Communism *has* brought equality—the equality of slavery. It has resulted in *inequality* in the amount of work a woman is required to do. *U.S. News & World Report* reported on the status of women in Russia by noting, "Under the 1977 Constitution, men and women enjoy equal political status, equal pay for equal work, and access to jobs with no discrimination between the sexes. But the stark realities bear little resemblance to the legal guarantees."[11]

Many wives and divorced mothers must work at least eight hours a day at their jobs, then come home and spend more than thirty hours a week on household chores. Men spend only fifteen hours a week doing housework. Moreover, Russian women are not blessed with all of the labor-saving devices we have. There are only 67 washing machines per 100 families and only 68 refrigerators per 100 families.[12] Many women, even those living just outside Moscow, must wash their clothes in ponds.[13]

Soviet women constitute 40 percent of those engaged in hard manual labor, and the figure is continuing to rise.[14] Women are found predominantly in the lower paying jobs, working as clerks, typists, or saleswomen.

Easy divorce in Russia and the severe economic hardships of women have resulted in a hardened attitude toward marriage. According to *U.S. News*, "Soviet morality bans pornography and the striptease. Yet it is tolerant of free love and has generated a somewhat frivolous attitude toward marriage. Divorces are easy for those with no children, so couples sometimes wed just to be together on organized, state-subsidized vacations. Young men will marry Moscow spinsters to obtain the necessary official papers allowing them to reside in the capital."[15]

Soviet officials are alarmed at the falling birthrate, but women know that the more children they have, the harder life will be for them. So they abort their children. It's not unusual for a Soviet woman to have as many as six abortions during her lifetime.[16]

The dismal situation in Russia is nothing new. As soon as the Communists seized power, they began putting Marxist principles into action to abolish the family. One of the first things the Soviets did was to abolish the term "illegitimate children," thus equalizing the status of all children, whether born within marriage or outside it. Then they simplified divorce proceedings, reducing the whole process to a matter of minutes.

Easy divorce brought total disruption in Russian society. A woman who saw this collapse of the family firsthand detailed her observations in the July 1926 issue of *Atlantic Monthly*. She noted that because of easy divorce, "Chaos was the result. Men took to changing wives with the same zest which they displayed in the consumption of the recently restored forty-percent vodka."[17] One Russian woman complained to the author that some men "have twenty wives, living a week with one, a month with another."[18]

Children born out of these casual associations were simply discarded as men went from one wife to another. These little ones ended up on the streets. "They are one of the greatest social dangers of the present time, because they are developing into professional criminals. More than half of them are drug addicts and sex perverts."[19]

Men were not the only ones to exploit the ease of

getting a divorce. Many women decided to make a profit by having children. They would seduce sons of wealthy peasants and then blackmail the fathers for support payments.

Efforts to abolish the traditional "bourgeois" family also created problems in economic productivity. "During the winter of 1924–1925 some of the older Communists accused the younger generation, especially the students, of indulging in too much dissipation, of squandering health and vitality in loose connections; they blamed the girl students of practicing frequent abortions."[20] The Communists were alarmed that the youth were going to spend all their time engaging in "free love" instead of helping to "build the socialist state."

Little has changed in Russia since those early years. Men and women are still enslaved under a totalitarian system, and women are burdened with the double obligation of working in the world and caring for the household. One American feminist observed, "Russian women have the worst of both worlds. They have the legislation, but they aren't liberated. They are obligated to work and have lost the choice of being home-makers."[21]

CHINESE COMMUNISM AND WOMEN

Before the Communists assumed power in China, the family had been the most important unit of society. Franklin House writes in *A History of Chinese Communism* that the family "assumed the primary responsibility for providing shelter, food, and love for its members, rearing the young and caring for the old. It was the molder of personal conduct, the transmitter of technical skills and everyday wisdom, the custodian of traditional values, beliefs, customs and habits, and the strongest magnet of loyalty."[22]

In pre-Communist days, Chinese culture was ruled by the wisdom of Confucius. One author has noted, "Confucius put the woman below the man, but he tempered this with the status of generation and age, and mellowed it with harmony between the spouses. The Chinese woman was far more influential than Western sociological legends would have us believe, since she received filial obeisance. Even before her husband she was not necessarily a picture of submissiveness."[23]

Women exercised an inordinate amount of power in China through a network of family associations of wives, aunts, and mothers. "Look into Chinese history and one finds behind every throne a delicate female hand."[24]

When the Communists took control of China, one of their first acts was to institute the Marriage Law. Promulgated on April 30, 1950, this law banned arranged and child marriages, the sale of children, and polygamy. It also gave widows the right to remarry and all women equal rights with men to work.[25]

Mao Tse-tung wrote, "In order to build a great socialist society, it is of the utmost importance to arouse the broad masses of women to join in productive activity. Men and women must receive equal pay for equal work in production. Genuine equality between the sexes can only be realized in the process of the socialist transformation of society as a whole."[26]

Under the Marriage Law, divorce was encouraged as a way of dissolving bourgeois marriages. Unfortunately many women couldn't cope with this new "freedom" and chose suicide instead. From May 1950 to July 1951, more than 10,000 women killed themselves rather than be pressured into getting divorces.[27]

Not only were women forced into getting divorces, but many peasant girls were required to marry Communist party officials or be brutalized. Many were "raped by Communist officials to whom they went for marriage licenses. In three cities and fourteen counties in Kwangtung, 1,024 murders and suicides took place in 20 months because of marital and sexual troubles."[28]

According to Communist records, 70,000 to 80,000

persons, mostly women, died each year as a result of this new directive for the bourgeois family. Illegitimacy was rampant, and statistics revealed, for example, that in one county alone more than 1,800 babies were drowned in a year.[29]

Chinese women achieved "equality of opportunity" all right. "In 1952 only 30 percent of the peasant women worked in the fields. By 1958 over 90 percent were doing hard labor, of whom 73 million worked in water conservancy, 67 million in forestation, and 13 million in experimental farming. By making menstruating and pregnant women pull plows, dig ditches, and haul stone, the average annual working days for women were doubled within two years. Many miscarriages resulted."[30]

Life in Communist China is no easier today. Women who become pregnant after having one child are treated as criminals. Under Marxist laws it is now a crime against the state to have more than one child. If a woman who already has a child gets pregnant again, she will be forced to undergo an abortion. In Guangdong province, Communist officials are cracking down on the "crime" of becoming pregnant. According to a *New York Times* dispatch of May 16, 1982, "Local legislation augmenting the national family planning directives has given Guangdong some of the strongest incentives and penalties in China. Late marriages are encouraged, for example, and students who marry face expulsion from school."[31]

Parents who have only one child are given priority in housing and medical care and receive free kindergarten service. Women who have gotten pregnant are often "abducted, handcuffed, or trussed to abortion clinics." Others are hauled into detention camps or made to stand in front of mass rallies and harangued into getting abortions.

A former anthropology student from Stanford University spent a year in China studying local culture. Steven

W. Mosher was stunned to see women being hauled off to have abortions. He took photographs of the procedures and published them in the *Sunday Times Chinese Weekly* in Taiwan. As a result of his pursuit of truth, Stanford University expelled the student from its graduate program. According to an Associated Press dispatch, Mosher stated that forced abortions were performed in at least twelve counties in the region of the Pearl River Delta in southern China. "All women of child-bearing age were ordered in for pelvic examinations," Mosher said. "Women were required to attend clinics every six months and alternately threatened and persuaded over several days or weeks to submit to abortions and tubal ligations to prevent future pregnancies."[32]

In 1981, according to available statistics, more than 600,000 abortions were performed among the 7,000,000 women of childbearing age in Guangdong province.[33]

Communist China, like Communist Russia, has promised women "equality." What have they received? The Marxist system has given them equality of misery, slavery, and death.

We should look to the Russian and Chinese models of "equality of opportunity" to get a picture of where America's feminists are leading us. We could find ourselves with the same kind of liberation that women have in totalitarian empires.

In this survey of how women are treated in other lands, we can see two extreme viewpoints. In some countries a woman is kept from participating in society by being secluded in her home. In others, women are not just given the opportunity to work, they are *required* to do so. In most developing nations women work because economically they have no choice. In none of these countries does a woman receive the kind of love, honor, and courtesy she once received in our country. I say *once* received, because "women's liberation" has brought about a trend toward demeaning womanhood and an end to chivalry. Feminism has caused an unnatural division between men and women. Today men are often afraid to act as gentlemen in opening doors or offering their seats to women. To be a gentleman, they risk being clubbed on the head by an irate "woman's libber." So many men have stopped treating women with courtesy.

Our Lord never intended women to live as hermits within the confines of the home, but neither does He expect women to neglect their families so they can pursue their careers. Between the two extremes of seclusion and careerism, there is a happy medium. I think God would have all women look for that middle ground, and there find contentment.

It's important to look at modern-day feminists and see what kind of world they are offering us. In the press they claim to speak for the women of America. In reality they speak only for themselves, wishing to impose their views on the majority of women who want to be good wives and mothers.

Granted, there is discontentment among American women. But what the feminists offer as solutions have already been tried in Russia and China. If the feminists succeed, women here could be living under the same kind of tyranny that Russian and Chinese women are experiencing today.

NOTES

[1] Denise L. Carmody, *Women and World Religions* (Nashville, Tenn.: Abingdon, 1975), 45.

[2] "Women in Crisis," World Vision International Telethon (September 1982).

[3] Janet Z. Giele and Audrey C. Smock, eds., *Women—Roles and Status in Eight Countries* (New York, N.Y.: John Wiley & Sons, 1977), 87.

[4] Carmody, *Women and World Religions*, 145.

[5] Giele and Smock, *Women—Roles and Status in Eight Countries*, 39.

[6] "Women in Crisis," World Vision International Telethon.

[7] Ibid.

[8] Mary Daly, *Gyn/Ecology* (Boston, Mass.: Beacon Press, 1978), 160.

[9] Carmody, *Women and World Religions*, 34.

[10] Giele and Smock, *Women—Roles and Status in Eight Countries*, 142.

[11] "For Russia's Women, Worst of Both Worlds," *U.S. News & World Report* (June 28, 1982): 53.

[12] "Soviet Union: The Role of Women," *Washington Times* (August 23, 1982): 8A.

[13] "For Russia's Women, Worst of Both Worlds," 53.

[14] "Soviet Union: The Role of Women," 8A.

[15] "For Russia's Women, Worst of Both Worlds," 53.

[16] Ibid., 54.

[17] "The Russian Effort to Abolish Marriage," *Atlantic Monthly* (July 1926): 108.

[18] Ibid.

[19] Ibid.

[20] Ibid., 108, 110.

[21] "For Russia's Women, Worst of Both Worlds," 54.

[22] Franklin House, *A History of Chinese Communism* (Englewood Cliffs, N.J.: Prentice-Hall, 1967), 180.

[23] Valentin Chu, *Ta Ta, Tan Tan* (New York: W. W. Norton, 1963), 132.

[24] Ibid.

[25] House, *A History of Chinese Communism*, 180.

[26] "Women Have Gone to the Labour Front," *The Socialist Upsurge in China's Countryside*, Communist Chinese edition, vol. 1 (1955).

[27] House, *A History of Chinese Communism*, 182.

[28] Chu, *Ta Ta, Tan Tan*, 130.

[29] Ibid.

[30] Ibid.

[31] "Chinese Region Showing Resistance to National Goals for Birth Control," *New York Times* (May 16, 1982): Y29.

[32] "Stanford Expels Graduate Student," *Santa Ana Register* (February 25, 1983).

[33] "Chinese Region Showing Resistance," Y29.

5.

Women in the
Wrong Direction

The "restless woman" is confused about who she is and what she should be doing with her life. If she's married, she isn't quite sure she wants to be a housewife or mother. Often what she sees on television or reads in women's magazines seems to tell her that she's "trapped" and "unproductive" if she stays at home. Many of her friends have "escaped" from their homes and are working full-time. They wear expensive clothing and go on business trips. Their lives seem to be much more exciting than the life of a "housewife." From all outward appearances career women seem to have achieved success and status in the world.

The wife and/or mother who chooses to stay at home doesn't possess that sort of worldly "status." Often she feels like a nonentity. She almost feels ashamed if she has to tell someone what she does. She may say, "Oh, I'm *just* a housewife." She's embarrassed to admit that she takes care of the home and children. She feels inferior because she's not a computer programmer, business executive, or scientist.

After I spoke at a women's conference in the Midwest, a young, attractive lady with two young daughters was waiting in line to speak with me. I could not help but notice her two blond, curly-headed children, for they looked as if they had stepped out of a magazine ad.

As she drew near, her first words were, "Mrs. LaHaye, I don't feel like I am fulfilling my potential in life." She had overlooked the fact that training and developing good character traits in two lovely daughters was the greatest challenge she could have at this stage of her life. Her question to me should have been, "How can I help fulfill the potential of my daughters' lives when there are so many forces working against me?" Her focus was on the wrong person—which is a common problem in the restless woman.

Feminists often consider this kind of woman worthless and unproductive. She gets no encouragement from the mass media. Many of her friends are working full-time, so she becomes isolated and resentful. If she's a churchgoer, she may receive little support from the church. The truth is, many church women have also decided to find "fulfillment" outside the home.

WHAT DO RESTLESS WOMEN WANT?

What do these restless women want? Several years ago I read a newspaper article recounting a meeting of the National Council of Jewish Women in Nashville, Tennessee. The keynote speaker was Shirley Leviton, and the title of her speech was "What Does a Woman Want?" Here's what Mrs. Leviton said: "Even though I've been researching the feminine soul for the thirty years I've been active in the NCJW, I've not yet been able to answer the question of what women want."[1]

That's not a very encouraging answer. This woman has been studying women for thirty years, yet she's just as befuddled as ever.

She's not alone in her confusion. Other women are saying the same thing. Judith M. Bardwick, a feminist, has written one of the fairest and most honest analyses of the woman's problem I've come across. In the first chapter of her book, *In Transition,* she candidly admits, "I have no prescriptions for happiness."[2]

The restless woman is desperately searching for some sense of identity and meaning for existence. She needs to be loved by her husband and children. She needs to know she matters in their lives. She needs her own identity and sense of self-worth. She's restless at home because she has been led to believe she's not contributing anything worthwhile to society. She needs to change her emphasis on self and consider others.

But several factors have conspired against her. For the most part, she's been cut loose from her religious beliefs, so she has to work out her problems without the help of God. If she's like most wives and mothers, she's probably made several moves as her husband changed jobs. As a result, she's been cut off from her family relationships and childhood friends. She doesn't feel as if she belongs anywhere. She has no sense of stability. She may have been rejected by her husband and now has to face life alone. Because of the philosophy of the "libbers" that tells women that marriage is like imprisonment and they are under bondage, it is no longer uncommon for the wife to be the one to turn her back on the spouse.

The dilemma of the modern woman is not new. Women have been facing a sense of restlessness since the Industrial Revolution brought about significant changes in the nature and structure of the family.

One feminist writer accurately observes, "Industrialization, particularly with the development of steam power, led to a rapid growth in cities and marked the shift in the nature of population from rural to urban. The consequences of this at first were disastrous, not so much for attitudes toward women, but in the social functions of women. As industry moved into the factory, a wife for a workingman was no longer an economic asset but more likely a liability, while children could prove economic disasters."[3]

In our agricultural society, the typical family was a closely knit economic unit. The father, mother, and children were all intimately involved in the jobs of survival and production. There was mutual dependence on each other. But as mass production became commonplace, fathers more frequently went off to the factory to earn a living.

This created a separation between husbands and wives and children. The father became the "breadwinner," the mother became a "homemaker," and the children went off to school. There had been spiritual strength in the agrarian family unit. One author has written, "The traditional family exemplifies a well-known sociological principle that love and affection tend to develop between people who work together according to some division of labor which forces them to become dependent on one another."[4]

That strength dissipated as the husband left the family business and went to work in town. In *Our Dance Has Turned to Death*, Carl Wilson writes, "...The main problem of the decline of the family in America lies in the fact that men have forsaken their responsibility for spiritual leadership and under self-deception have departed from practicing faith in God. The pivotal point in the man's failure is evidenced by the change from the worship of God to the worship of mammon."[5]

The urbanization of our society broke down an important interdependency between husband and wife. She became dependent on him for her survival. In his quest for material wealth, the husband neglected his family and his spiritual responsibilities as the head of the family unit.

Where the home was once the center of economic activity for the family, it was gradually stripped of many of its functions. The woman no longer has to sew clothing, make soap, or preserve fruit and vegetables. The many labor-saving devices available to women has made life "easier," but has also brought new problems: what does woman do with her leisure time? It no longer takes a woman eight-to-ten hours a day to keep up with the daily tasks of homemaking; she now has spare time. The special, creative "art of homemaking" is being lost to the idea that homemaking is drudgery and routine.

The home was also stripped of its educational function when children were required to attend public schools. Even the Sunday school movement played a part, for it relieved nominal Christians of the need to teach their children about the Lord. In the agrarian society, mothers were the ones who taught their children about the world around them; mothers transmitted cultural and moral values to their children. This important function has largely been replaced by public schooling.

In a very real sense the "home" is an extension of the mother's womb, a place where nurturing takes place. Yet, as the mother's economic and educational functions were taken away, she became restless and dissatisfied with the life she was leading. Her husband, caught up in the mad race for material wealth, had more important priorities than his wife and children, and this added to her anguish. He was more concerned about his job than his family. For too many American families, instead of the home being a "womb"—a place of security, comfort and love—it has become a place where family members eat and sleep. Loving, binding communication has almost vanished.

Many homes are no longer training grounds for children or a place where family members learn to work together and love each other. One author notes, "The destruction of the traditional home has been emotionally hazardous to men, women, and children. But it has affected no one more destructively than women and is the root cause of modern women's restlessness and discontent, shown in so many ways."[6]

With her husband spending long hours at work and

her children running off to pursue their own interests, the modern woman finds herself at home with little or nothing to keep her occupied. Her anxiety is understandable. She sees her family out finding "self-fulfillment," so why shouldn't she do likewise? She finds herself unsure of her purpose in life and feeling empty and deserted. Should she spend her leisure hours at the health club or watching soap operas? The tragedy is that many women turn to alcohol to rid themselves of their anxieties. Yet that only creates additional problems. And if she gets a job outside the home, she often goes on a guilt-trip, torn between her obligations at home and her occupation. She can't seem to reconcile them in her mind and ends up doing a bad job at both. What she needs most of all is to be respected and loved for *who she is*—not *what she does*. Moreover, she desperately needs to turn her focus toward her family rather than herself.

If she's interested in staying up on current events and reads women's magazines, she finds that they give her no emotional support. Take an honest look at the women's magazines on the market; most of them are merely serving feminist purposes. They are propaganda tools of those who are antiman, antifamily, and anti-God.

Cosmopolitan magazine, for example, is probably the most socially destructive. It advocates an immoral lifestyle for women. The "Cosmo" girl is encouraged to be as promiscuous as men are in *Playboy* magazine. In the May 1983 issue of *Cosmopolitan* there is an article entitled "How to Have Sex If You're Not Human," by Mary Batten. After describing the sex life of various animals and plants around the world, Miss Batten says, "Rather than being degrading, as some religious fundamentalists believe, human kinship with the apes and other animals and plants is wondrous—a stunning demonstration of the biochemical bonds linking all forms of life on Earth. . . . By broadening our perspective on sex to include its biological roots in the rest of the living world, we may achieve true sexual liberation. We can take the guilt-ridden ghosts from the closet, sweep out the tangled webs of Freudian fantasies, and simply have fun. We may be the only animals who can!"[7]

In that same issue is an article entitled "What Makes You Say YES to a Man?" The writer compiled several comments from "liberated" women, telling why they are willing to have sexual intercourse with a man. These women gave a variety of responses, all of which trivialize the sex act. What were their reasons? One said she would bed down with a man if she liked the way he kissed. Another had sex because her boyfriend had given her roses. One woman said, "Sometimes I'll have sex just for the adventure. I recall a brief, passionate fling I had with a married man. It was tempestuous and tearful but more *diverting* than a trip to the world's most exotic locale!" Other reasons: revenge; the smell of his aftershave lotion; greed; foreign accents; nostalgia.[8]

Cosmopolitan and similar magazines are not providing any solutions for the restless woman. They *are*, however, sowing seeds of discontent among women and giving many moral-minded women an inferiority complex. Magazines such as *Self* and *Ebony* are also profeminist and antifamily in their articles. An article entitled "Should You Bring Your Toothbrush & Diaphragm?" in *Self* magazine, for instance, counsels young women on the art of "making love." The author cautions, "The most important subject to get out of the way, unpleasant as it is to contemplate, is that of sexually transmitted diseases."[9]

Ebony magazine promotes sexual immorality among black women. In "Sexual Freedom and the 'Now' Woman," the author says, "In our own minds, we're rejecting the stereotypes and the myths that shackled us, the roles that limited us; those who are thinking aren't about to claim an X-rated image. Why trade one set of chains for another? The true sexual revolution is a positive fusion of sexuality with self-awareness, assertiveness with personal responsibility and, yes, control."[10]

The restless woman faces some real problems, but she will not find any helpful answers in women's magazines. A woman who is constantly filling her mind with what is in these magazines will find herself becoming more and more discontent; she will become more dissatisfied with her life; she will be more likely to discard her husband and children to chase elusive fantasies. Little is said in most women's magazines about commitment or responsibility in a marriage relationship; little is said about the deep psychological damage done to children as a result of divorce.

SELF-FULFILLMENT

A major theme in feminist writings is the concept of self-fulfillment. This is supposed to be the main concern of all men and women. If they aren't "fulfilled" in a marriage relationship, they should quit, according to feminist reasoning. If a woman is unhappy at home with a baby, she should simply deposit the child in a day-care center so she can pursue her goal of self-fulfillment and "happiness." If she gets pregnant at an inconvenient time in her life, she should have the baby aborted. Or if she gives birth to a malformed baby, she should have the option of putting the child on a shelf in the hospital until it starves to death. The whole theme of this philosophy is to take charge of yourself, even if it is destructive of others.

Judith Bardwick has well stated, "Contemporary feminism reflects our culture's general drift toward the legitimacy, even the priority, of egocentric hedonism."[11] It doesn't surprise me that restless women are following in the footsteps of modern men. Far too many men have adopted the so-called Playboy Philosophy, which is an adolescent view of sex. Hugh Hefner and others of his ilk have spent nearly three decades teaching men that women are sex objects who exist only for their pleasure. These men have been conditioned to look at women not as human beings but as sex organs. They have been taught that men and women should engage in sexual intercourse any time they wish, married or not. Fidelity in marriage is irrelevant. Through pornographic magazines, men are taught that materialism and the conquest of women are the most important goals in life. Women are simply pleasure machines to be used, abused, and discarded.

Women are being taught the same thing in women's magazines, not just in *Cosmopolitan,* but also in such pornographic magazines as *Playgirl.* Men are also being viewed as sex objects. Women are chasing materialism and sex, just as men do. Will this really solve the dilemma of the restless woman? *I know it won't.* No woman is going to find true happiness or contentment by pursuing egocentric hedonism. Lust is insatiable; the more you seek to fulfill your lust for "things" or sex, the more you must have. Living the kind of life described in these women's magazines will only lead to broken hearts, venereal disease, and spiritual death. The restless woman needs more than a fancy wardrobe and a series of one-night stands. Her most basic emotional needs must be fulfilled. But what do the feminists offer as a solution to her anxiety?

ANOTHER WORLDVIEW

As a Christian believing in the reality of Jesus Christ, I have a Christian worldview. The Bible is the Word of God given to teach us and train us. It gives us a standard of morality.

There is, however, another worldview. Those who reject Christ or are not aware of His reality in their lives live by another set of moral standards such as "situation ethics" or some other man-made ethical system. In my opinion, these people are living in rebellion against

God's laws, no matter how wonderful their ethical system may seem to be.

There are, then, just two worldviews: the Christian and the non-Christian. The humanist-feminists, as evidenced in their writings, reject the reality of God and Jesus Christ and Christian moral principles. In essence they are teaching a humanistic worldview: morality is whatever you wish it to be.

An example of this view of morality is found in *Ebony* magazine: "Often the changing sexual times touch on morality. It's clear that more single women are having affairs with married men, and more married women are engaging in triangles of their own. Because of the gay and women's movements, lesbian relationships, deemed by some as immoral, have become more open. Many women choose living together over marriage. It's official: if it feels good, do it."[12]

The essence of the sexual revolution in America during the past twenty-to-thirty years is *If it feels good, do it*. That attitude has been applied mainly to sexual relations between men and women, but it has also infected the family. A cult of selfishness has grown up in America that may destroy our civilization. In any bookstore you can find rows and rows of books declaring your "right" to be arrogant, self-centered, egotistical, and intimidating. No family will survive long if each of its members adopts the philosophy of "doing your own thing." Within each family there must be an environment of mutual caring, love, and dependency or it will simply fall apart.

Betty Friedan and The Feminine Mystique

Feminists have catered to the restless woman's natural desire for meaning and self-fulfillment. Betty Friedan, for example, is considered to be the "mother" of the twentieth-century feminist movement. Her book *The Feminine Mystique*, published in 1963, laid the groundwork for the radical feminist movement. Her basic theme was this: housewives are trapped in their homes with nothing to do; the only way they can truly be liberated and fulfilled is to find work in the world. It was Friedan's belief that for a woman to be fully human, she had to compete with men in the working world.

Ten years after writing *The Feminine Mystique*, Betty Friedan became a signer of the *Humanist Manifesto II*, written by Paul Kurtz and Edwin H. Wilson. This manifesto presents an anti-God philosophy. It also states, "In the area of sexuality, we believe that intolerant attitudes, often cultivated by orthodox religions and puritanical cultures, unduly repress sexual conduct. The right to birth control, abortion, and divorce should be recognized."[13]

Betty Friedan is working for the establishment of a humanist society devoid of Christianity. She is seeking to bring about an American culture where the traditional family would be obsolete. The family of the future would be "two or more persons who share resources, share responsibility for decisions, share values and goals, and have commitments to one another over time. The family is that climate that one 'comes home to' and it is this network of sharing and commitments that most accurately describes the family unit, regardless of blood, legal ties, adoption, or marriage."[14]

A 1983 issue of *U.S. News & World Report* offers an ominous vision of what the future family may be like: "Over the next five decades, experts say, society will redefine its concept of the family. Through the pattern of divorce and remarriage, a whole new network of kinship will arise. There will be double sets of grandparents, aunts, uncles, and brothers and sisters, as well as former in-laws and ex-spouses—all of them making up the new divorce-extended family. . . . Beyond the traditional unit of Mom, Pop and the kids, sociologists see a growth of nonfamily-type households—group marriages, gay parents, unmarried couples, communes of close friends, and a growing number of single parents."[15]

That is the kind of future Betty Friedan is working toward. In her book *The Second Stage* she outlines her hopes for the future of the feminist movement. It is not only equal pay for equal work that concerns her. She is actively seeking a total transformation of society into a socialist-humanist state.

Among the prominent feminists in the United States, however, she is presented as a "moderate," a woman of calm restraint. Beside the radicals she *does* look like a moderate, but she is probably the more dangerous because her writings seem so reasonable, logical, and necessary.

Like many of the nineteenth-century feminists, Betty Friedan is the product of a disrupted home life. She admits that her feminism arose out of her mother's rebellion against being forced to quit her job as a newspaper editor when she married Betty's father. Her mother's rebellion carried over into the marriage. "Her activities and energies," says Betty, "kept my father feeling continually inadequate and on the edge of bankruptcy, because no matter how much he made, it wasn't enough for her."[16] Her mother, embittered that she couldn't earn her own way, began gambling, continually lost, and engaged in endless battles with her husband. "She was not a happy housewife. Her ulcerating colitis, which forced her to bed in sickening agony for days at a time, only subsided when my father's heart trouble and premature invalidism and death made it necessary for her to take over and run his business."[17]

Betty Friedan was victimized by her parents. She had a weak-willed father who failed to exercise his proper authority in the family and a domineering, scheming mother. That combination will often produce emotionally disturbed children. Psychoanalyst Harold Voth writes, "The effect on children when their father is not a strong, masculine man and their mother a strong, feminine woman, when a strong family bond fails to exist, or when families disintegrate defies estimation. The cycle of sick or weak people who are the product of sick or broken families keeps repeating itself, the effects spread from one generation to the next and slowly but surely the sickness tears down the best traditions of mankind which made our society strong."[18]

In being deprived of a healthful home environment, Betty Friedan was early infected by the rebellion of her mother. She obviously has never overcome her hatred of her father for his failure to maintain order in his family. Children who grow up in an environment where the parents are always in conflict will not be able to have healthy relationships with others. In many cases these children will project their hatred of parental authority onto society as a whole, blaming "capitalism" or "patriarchy" for all social problems.

Ferdinand Lundberg and Marynia Farnham observe that the basis of the feminist movement is neurotic behavior, manifesting itself through hatred and rebellion. The cause of the neuroses? Parents. They write, "The general rule therefore is: Only insufficiently loving parents give rise to neurotics."[19]

The Bible states that the sins of the fathers fall upon their children and grandchildren (Exod. 20:5). I don't know what kind of upbringing Betty Friedan's parents had, but obviously neither one had helpful role models. As a result of their own inadequacies and sins, they passed on their personality flaws to Betty—and she has become a national leader—infecting millions with her personal problems.

Dr. Voth has dealt with thousands of men and women like Betty Friedan—people from wrecked homes. In his expert opinion, the ideal family is one in which "the father should be loving, compassionate, understanding, capable of gentleness, and the like—but all should know he is the protector, the one who is ultimately responsible for the integrity and survival of the family.

It is known that the most successful families are those where all members, including the wife, look up to the father-husband."[20]

Gloria Steinem and MS. Magazine

Gloria Steinem is another feminist leader whose life at home was chaotic and unnatural. Her grandmother, Pauline Steinem, was an early feminist who "served as president of the Ohio Women's Suffrage Association from 1908 to 1911 and was one of two United States delegates to the 1908 meeting of the International Council of Women."[21]

Gloria's father was an itinerant antique dealer, a ne'er-do-well who uprooted his family every few years as he wandered the country in search of fortune. Gloria once told a *Time* magazine interviewer, "He was always going to make a movie, or cut a record, or start a new hotel, or come up with a new orange drink."[22] Her parents were divorced when she was ten years old, and subsequently she lived with her mother in a rat-infested tenement in Toledo, Ohio.

She entered Smith College, a feminist-oriented women's college, and graduated magna cum laude in 1956 with a Phi Beta Kappa key and a degree in government. According to *Current Biography*, she spent two years in India and returned to America to become director of "the Independent Research Service in Cambridge, Massachusetts, a partially CIA-funded offshoot of the National Student Association. For that organization she rallied American students to attend Communist Youth festivals in Europe and directed a press service for foreign journalists."[23]

In 1964 and 1965 she was a scriptwriter for the National Broadcasting Company for the television program "That Was the Week that Was." In 1972 she launched *MS.* magazine, receiving financial and promotional help from *New York* magazine. Later Warner Communications took over financing the magazine. The purpose of *MS.*, Gloria said, was to serve as a "how-to" magazine, "for the liberated female human being—not how to make jelly but how to seize control of your life."[24]

Gloria Steinem has been one of the most vocal and active feminists in the country. Her view of the American family is evident in this comment: "Overthrowing capitalism is too small for us. We want to overthrow the whole f***** patriarchy."[25] And in a booklet entitled "What Is Now?" she says, "By the year 2000, we will, I hope, raise our children to believe in human potential, not God."[26]

Mary Calderone and Sex Education

Mary Calderone has taken a leading role in promoting promiscuous sex among teenagers in America. In large measure her organization, Sex Information and Education Council of the United States (SIECUS), has been responsible for encouraging teenagers to engage in free sex. The result has been millions of unwanted pregnancies and an epidemic of venereal disease. A hardcore feminist, Mary is the daughter of the renowned photographer Edward Steichen, famous for the *Family of Man* exhibit. She is also the product of a poor home life.

Mary's mother deserted Edward, taking one daughter with her and leaving Mary at the mercy of her traveling father. Mary has admitted, "What insecurities I had arose from the fact that my mother had removed herself from me at a very early age—my parents were separated—and I had no real home. I was sort of farmed out, and even though it was to loving friends, it made me very insecure emotionally . . . but I never doubted that someday I would find what I wanted to do and do it."[27] Torn from her mother at an early age and then deserted by her selfish father as he traveled all over the world, Mary Calderone is another example of a woman filled with anger and rebellion. She too has infected millions with her own kind of neurosis.

Dr. Onalee McGraw writes, "What Mary Calderone did in her adult life was to promote her vision of the new sexual orthodoxy of self-fulfillment. Is it really surprising that someone as intelligent and determined as this woman would overcome the painful withdrawal of parental love in childhood by proclaiming the message that sexuality is more important than familial values?"[28]

Andrea Dworkin

One of the most rabid man-haters among the feminists is Andrea Dworkin, author of numerous books dealing with pornography and women's issues. Dworkin's view of the world is severely distorted by a Marxian-Lesbian bias. In her book *Right-Wing Women,* she contends that women *in general* are hated by men *in general.*

She honestly believes that "right-wing" women have decided that the only way they can survive in a sexist society is to give in to the desires of men. Right-wing women, Dworkin says, use sex and have babies in order to remain valuable to men. They sell out to the patriarchal establishment in order to survive. Dworkin wants to destroy the patriarchal society, not compromise with it. Lesbianism seems to be the only alternative she can offer women.

She favorably quotes Victoria Woodhull as a woman of deep insight and maintains that "Feminism is a much-hated political philosophy. This is true all along the male-defined, recognizable political spectrum from far right to the left. Feminism is hated because women are hated. . . . This is because feminism is the liberation movement of women."[29]

Andrea Dworkin and others of her persuasion have declared war on what they view as an oppressive, male-dominated society. She says, "Facing the true nature of the sex-class system means ultimately that one must destroy that system or accommodate to it. Facing the true nature of male power over women also means that one must destroy that power or accommodate to it. Feminists, from a base of powerlessness, want to destroy that power; right-wing women, from a base of powerlessness, the same base, accommodate to that power because quite simply they see no way out from under."[30]

THE GOAL: A NEW ORDER IN SOCIETY

Betty Friedan, Gloria Steinem, Mary Calderone, and Andrea Dworkin are four of the better-known leaders of the feminist and sexual revolutions. They all say the same thing, some more tactfully than others. It is their belief that women must be liberated from home and children if they are to be truly human or truly free.

To achieve this goal, the liberated woman is working to restructure both our economic system and our family arrangements. She must have access to twenty-four-hour child-care services; she must be given special privileges at work; she must be given government subsidies; she must be allowed to destroy her unwanted children; if she is a lesbian, she must have the freedom to adopt children or to be artificially inseminated through a "gay" sperm bank; she must be granted the right to marry another woman if she desires; she must have the right to be a combat soldier, even if she can't possibly compete with men in physical strength.

These are just some of the sick ideas espoused by the leaders of the feminist movement. These women are the tragic victims of parental neglect. They have grown up filled with paranoia and impulsive hatred that drives them relentlessly toward their goals.

In a very real sense, these women are mentally disturbed. They developed these emotional difficulties because they failed to receive love and discipline in their homes. They no longer have to repress their anger; they can vent it against all of society. Dr. Voth has observed that most emotionally disturbed people usually try to alter their environment rather than change their behavior and admit they have emotional problems.

Child pornographers, known to law enforcement officers as "pedophiles," seldom admit they need help. Instead of seeking professional psychiatric assistance, they form their own political/social organizations such as the North American Man-Boy Lovers Association. These organizations *reinforce* the psychopathic behavior of these men, giving them justification to continue in their sexual abuse of preadolescent children.

This same tendency holds true in feminist organizations. Dr. Voth is alarmed at the organizational strength these women seem to possess in pushing their programs and legislation on the rest of us. He writes, "For society to endorse their antifemininity, their antifamily values, and their competitiveness with men is sheer nonsense. But worse than that, the movement places a stamp of acceptability or normality on what is, in fact, *a manifestation of psychiatric illness—that is, a social value which reflects the personal illness of a group of individuals.*" [31]

This kind of disturbed woman puts our society in grave danger. Voth goes on to say, "The picture is clear. Personal psychopathology has led to social pathology and laws are being passed which reinforce personal and social pathology." [32] In other words, these feminist leaders, most of whom seem to be in need of psychiatric help, have joined together to reinforce their own neuroses and then impose their notions of morality on the rest of us by lobbying for local, state, and federal legislation. They have joined together to overthrow our economic and social system. We cannot seriously consider valid what they say, but we *must* seriously oppose them in their efforts to destroy our culture. Onalee McGraw correctly observes that "those who are denied the love and nurturing that God intended the family to give may grow up to take their revenge on mankind." [33]

From Mary Wollenstonecraft to Betty Friedan, the

pattern is the same: love-starved women venting their rage against an entire civilization.

The restless woman will find no solace in joining the feminist movement. As one ex-feminist observed, "My abandonment of feminism was a process of intellect. It was also a process of observation. Look around and you'll see some happy women, and then you'll see these bitter, bitter women. The unhappy women are all feminists. You'll find very few happy, enthusiastic, relaxed people who are ardent supporters of feminism. Feminists are really tortured people."[34]

NOTES

[1] Virginia Keathley, "She's Still Searching for Women's Soul," *The Tennessean* (April 13, 1980):4E.

[2] Judith M. Bardwick, *In Transition* (New York: Holt, Rinehart and Winston, 1979), 8.

[3] Vern Bullough and Bonnie Bullough, *The Subordinate Sex—A History of Attitudes Toward Women* (Urbana, Ill.: Univ. of Illinois Press, 1973), 378.

[4] Genevieve De Hoyos, *Feminism or Familism?* (Provo, Utah: Northbridge, 1978), 66.

[5] Carl W. Wilson, *Our Dance Has Turned to Death* (Wheaton, Ill.: Tyndale House, 1981), 17.

[6] Ferdinand Lundberg and Marynia F. Farnham, *Modern Woman— The Lost Sex* (New York: Harper Brothers, 1947), 117.

[7] Mary Batten, "How to Have Sex If You're Not Human," *Cosmopolitan* (May 1983):304.

[8] Lynne Ames, "What Makes You Say YES to a Man?" *Cosmopolitan* (May 1983):177.

[9] Cheryl Merser, "Should You Bring Your Toothbrush & Diaphragm?" *Self* (May 1983):108.

[10] Bebe Moore Campbell, "Sexual Freedom and the 'Now' Woman," *Ebony* (August 1982):62.

[11] Bardwick, *In Transition*, 26.

[12] Campbell, "Sexual Freedom and the 'Now' Woman," 58.

[13] Paul Kurtz, ed., *Humanist Manifestoes I and II* (Buffalo: Prometheus, 1973), 18.

[14] Betty Friedan, *The Second Stage* (New York: Summit Books, 1981), 109.

[15] "When 'Family' Will Have a New Definition," *U.S. News & World Report* (May 9, 1983):A3-4.

[16] Friedan, *The Second Stage*, 93.

[17] Ibid.

[18] Harold M. Voth, *The Castrated Family* (Kansas City, Mo.: Universal Press Syndicate, 1977), xiii.

[19] Lundberg and Farnham, *Modern Woman—The Lost Sex*, 257.

[20] Voth, *The Castrated Family*, 4.

[21] "Gloria Steinem," *Current Biography* (1972):412.

[22] Ibid.

[23] Ibid.

[24] Ibid., 413.

[25] Gloria Steinem, *"What Is Now?"* (New York), 17.

[26] Ibid.

[27] Onalee McGraw, *The Family, Feminism and the Therapeutic State* (Washington: The Heritage Foundation, 1980), 26.

[28] Ibid.

[29] Andrea Dworkin, *Right-Wing Women* (New York: Perigee Books, G.P. Putnam's Sons, 1983), 195.

[30] Ibid., 236.

[31] Voth, *The Castrated Family*, 207.

[32] Ibid., 220.

[33] McGraw, *The Family, Feminism and the Therapeutic State*, 26.

[34] Susan Bolotin, "Voices From the Post-Feminist Generation," *New York Times Magazine* (October 17, 1982):29.

6.

The Root of Restlessness

The philosophy of rebellion and hatred underlying modern-day feminism has been largely responsible for the destruction of the American nuclear family. The feminist movement has drawn many restless women into its ranks—women who probably have legitimate gripes about the way they've been treated by men, but who are seeking answers to their problems in the wrong places.

Feminists are not rebelling only against what they call our "patriarchal society." They are actually rebelling against the unchangeable laws of God. As a result, our society is suffering from social disintegration. Being hardest hit is the basic unit of any society, the family.

The feminist and humanist philosophy of "doing your own thing" without any regard for God's moral laws has brought about an epidemic of venereal diseases, abortions, divorces, street crime, and untold anguish to millions of men, women, and children. Abortion clinics, psychiatric hospitals, divorce courts, and jails are filled with adults and youngsters who believed they could violate God's moral laws and not suffer the consequences. They have been lied to by the humanists and the feminists.

I want to make it clear that I am not singling out just

the feminist movement as the force destroying the family. Feminism and the sexual revolution are tentacles of the octopus Humanism, which is seeking to destroy Christianity and Christian principles in America.

The *Humanist Manifestoes I and II* call for the radical transformation of our society into an anti-God, amoral police state ruled by a humanist elite. Feminist, humanist, and Communist writings present the same message: All Christian principles must be destroyed; man is god; morality is relative. All three groups call for the destruction of capitalism as well as for sexual license.

The sexual revolution, which began quietly in the 1950s with the introduction of pornographic men's magazines, took a quantum leap during the mid-sixties. Anti-Vietnam War protesters, rock musicians, and drug culture leaders like Dr. Timothy Leary joined forces in a concerted effort to break down the traditional morality of American youth during those years.

Out of those terrible years came the frightening drug-abuse problem now threatening our society. Out of those rebellious years came the sexual revolution in which sex was no longer a sacred act of love between a man and wife but became a sport between "consenting adults." "Making love" was the euphemism used to describe the lustful act of fornicating with whoever might be available.

The sexual revolution has proved to be destructive, not only with lives ruined by venereal disease and abortions, but in terms of what used to be called "romance" between a man and a woman. Even liberals are finally admitting that couples must have more in common than a lustful desire for each other's bodies. Although they won't go so far as to admit that we should all live by the Christian virtues of virginity before marriage and fidelity in marriage, at least they are realizing that the "act of love" encompasses far more than the physical dimension. There are deep emotional needs that are unsatisfied when sex is trivialized.

George Leonard, author of *The End of Sex*, has written of the sexual revolution, "The trivialization of the erotic is most pronounced in 'recreational sex' in which sexual intercourse becomes a mere sport, divorced not only from love and creation, but also from empathy, compassion, morality, responsibility, and sometimes even common politeness."[1]

Leonard quotes a 1980 *Cosmopolitan* magazine survey of more than 106,000 women. The survey revealed in part, "So many readers wrote negatively about the sexual revolution, expressing longings for vanished intimacy and the now elusive joys of romance and commitment, that we began to sense that there might be a sexual counterrevolution under way in America."[2] Leonard admits that indiscriminate sex leads to the devaluation and depersonalization of relationships and of life itself.

An article published in *Psychology Today* also reports widespread disillusionment with the sexual revolution. Peter Marin writes, "Sexual life, which ought to begin with, and deepen, a pervasive and genuine sympathy between men and women, seems instead to produce among us a set of altogether different emotions: rage, disappointment, suspicion, antagonism, a sense of betrayal, and sometimes contempt. It is not so much that one cannot find good feelings in many persons or between many lovers; it is, rather, that the sexual realm as a whole seems somehow corrupted. . . . It remains for most men and women a world through which they move warily, cautiously, self-protectively—not a home but an alien land."[3]

The advocates of "sexual freedom" told us that once we discarded our outmoded, puritanical ideas about chastity, we would finally be "free" to enjoy sex. But this has not been the case, even among so-called swingers. The February 1983 issue of *Psychology Today* has an article titled "Swingers' Questionable Mental Health." Two Indiana psychologists analyzed members of a swingers sex club in the Midwest. More than half of the thirty members studied showed signs of psychopathology. "The swingers' most common problem was hypomania, a condition characterized by overactivity, over-optimism, and an emotional state that veers from euphoria to outbursts of temper. Other abnormal conditions included depression, a tendency to use physical problems as excuses for avoiding conflicts or responsibilities, and a basically cold, constrained, and sometimes deluded outlook."[4]

The humanists-feminists have taken a gift from God—the sacred relationship between a man and woman in marriage—and have dirtied it and emptied it of its spiritual significance in the lives of millions of men and women. In doing so, they have created a rift between men and women. Millions of men, driven by lust, inflamed by sexually exploitative movies and pornographic magazines, now look on women as "prey" rather than potential marriage partners. And many women are following their lead in their attitude toward men. Who could have imagined twenty years ago that a magazine as repulsive as *Playgirl* would have had a chance to succeed; or that women would flock to see male strippers at such places as Chippendales in Los Angeles?

It is little wonder that the practitioners of sexual freedom are growing weary of being hunted, used, and discarded. Perhaps they are learning, through bitter experience, that living by biblical morality assures healthier sexual relationships. In fact, a few years ago *Redbook* magazine conducted an extensive sexual survey of its readers. More than 100,000 women answered the questionnaire. The editors observed, "Sexual satisfaction is related significantly to religious belief. With notable consistency, the greater the intensity of a woman's religious convictions, the likelier she is to be highly satisfied with sexual pleasures of marriage. . . . This tendency exists among women of all ages."[5]

Restless women, whether or not they are feminists, would save themselves much sorrow if they obeyed the Bible, which is the Word of God. In it God has given us clear moral guidelines to live by. If we obey them, we will invariably be joyful, no matter what trials may come our way. Luke 11:28 tells us, "Blessed rather are those who hear the word of God and obey it." We can't ignore God's guidelines without suffering loss, whether mental or physical health. The Bible tells us we are to remain virgins until we marry. The sexual act itself is considered by God to be the "act of marriage" by which we become "one flesh" with a spouse. And marriage is a lifelong commitment. It is not something to be entered into lightly, yet the feminists have trivialized the institution of marriage along with the sex act.

In "Revolution: Tomorrow is NOW," a National Organization for Women publication, these radical feminists call for a "marriage contract" that can be renegotiated at intervals. They also call for a woman to have the right to refuse to take her husband's name in marriage. These feminists don't look at marriage as the union between two people who love and trust each other. Rather, they see marriage as a precarious business partnership, where the wife must always be protected from her husband by federal laws and social welfare workers. The husband is viewed as an oppressor, an enemy—not a loving provider.

VENEREAL DISEASES RAMPANT

One byproduct of the sexual revolution is the spread of various venereal diseases in our society. In 1977 there were more than 10 million reported cases of VD, 86 percent of them involving people fifteen to twenty-nine years old. The most common diseases: trichomoniasis, 3 million cases; gonorrhea, 2.5 million; NGU, 2.5 million; genital herpes, 300,000; syphilis, 25,000.[6]

According to an article in *Reader's Digest*, genital herpes has affected some 20 million Americans, with as many as "half a million new cases expected this year." Herpes researcher Dr. Kevin Murphy of Dallas has observed, "Today, if you are going to have sex, you are, to some degree, going to risk getting genital herpes."[7] Herpes can also be contracted apart from sexual activity, because researchers at UCLA have discovered that herpes viruses can live on toilet seats for as long as four hours.

At this writing there is no known cure for genital herpes. A victim will have it the rest of his life. Herpes is far more painful to women than to men, because more blisters appear. Also, women who have it may develop cancer of the cervix. Pregnant women who have herpes can transmit the disease to their children. According to Phyllis Schlafly, "Herpes is fatal to the majority of infected newborns. Of the babies who survive, half suffer blindness or brain damage."[8] Delivery by Caesarean section is advised for pregnant women with herpes.

Another venereal disease that is affecting women is pelvic inflammatory disease (PID). This disease often results from untreated gonorrhea. Each year more than 1 million women contract PID. According to *USA Today*, "Of those, 300,000 are hospitalized; half undergo surgery." PID can result in ovarian cysts, abscesses, infertility, ectopic pregnancy, and endometriosis.[9] It has also been discovered that women who use intrauterine devices (IUDs) run two-to-four times the risk of getting PID compared with women who use the barrier method of birth control. "The most prevalent and dangerous new infection that causes PID is non-gonococcal urethritis. Between 3 million and 4 million people contract this disease each year compared with about 2 million cases of gonorrhea. . . ."[10]

If men and women who engage in premarital sex did not have enough of a problem with herpes, gonorrhea, and PID, experts say that *mutant* strains of gonorrhea and PID, experts say that *mutant* strains of gonorrhea and chlamydia are now proliferating across the country. They are immune to penicillin or other standard antibiotics.

In her pamphlet *Herpes, Just the Facts,* Phyllis Schlafly presents a very simple solution to the venereal disease problem: "The best way to avoid getting Venereal Herpes is to avoid sexual relations. Remain a virgin until you marry, marry a virgin, and remain faithful to each other."[11] In other words, live by Christian principles as outlined in the Bible and you'll avoid the anguish facing more than twenty million men and women who are suffering with genital herpes. These men and women are just a few of the victims of the humanist-feminist-promoted sexual revolution. There are more, as we'll see.

ABORTION, AMERICAN STYLE

Ever since the 1973 Supreme Court decision legalizing the murder of unborn children, an average of 1.3 million mothers a year have chosen to kill their babies. This, according to feminist logic, is an exercise of their constitutional right to have control over their own bodies. While it is good that we lament the death of the 6 million Jews who were murdered in Hitler's concentration camps, we have neglected to mourn properly the death of some 15 million tiny human beings who have been "legally" and quietly murdered in antiseptic operating rooms and clinics all across this country.

We have no photographs of these tiny children staring at us from inside their concentration camps. We have no photographs of piles of tiny babies being shoveled into mass graves. We have seen the photos of mountains of Jewish bodies being bulldozed into lime pits. But American abortionists have been more sanitary with their murders. The corpses of baby boys and girls have been shredded and dropped into garbage cans or incinerators. Yet the horror of their deaths is still as real as the murder of six million Jews.

The "right" to kill unborn children has been a longtime goal of both feminists and humanists. They have achieved a legal right in the courts, but that does not—and will never—make it morally right to kill a helpless human being. We must remember that it was *lawful* in Germany to herd millions of Jews into the camps. It was legal to gas them; hang them on meat hooks; use them for cruel medical experiments; bury them alive. Under Nazi "law" all of these atrocities were "legal" and therefore "right."

Is this the kind of legal system we are under today in America? I believe it is. We are moving from the legalized murder of unborn babies to the legalization of infanticide and euthanasia. When will it stop? Only when we again live under a system of government that recognizes the reality of God and accepts His rule in our lives. The Bible teaches us that human life is sacred. We are to protect it, nourish it, and love it.

THE SOCIAL DESTRUCTIVENESS OF DIVORCE

In Malachi 2:16 God tells us how He views the marriage relationship: " 'I hate divorce,' says the Lord God of Israel."

God intended the marriage of a man and a woman to last a lifetime. God's ideal plan was to have them marry and be faithful to each other. Within the family they are to love each other and their children. They are to live productive lives, obey the laws of the land, be honest in their dealings, and share the gospel of Jesus Christ with others.

Today these principles are ignored by millions. The cost of "doing your own thing" is high. Feminists have been pushing for easy divorce for years and have succeeded. Millions of restless women and men have chosen to dissolve their marriage relationships rather than work at them. We live in a society that teaches us the "need" for instant gratification of our desires with "happiness" as our highest goal. Judith Bardwick has called it "egocentric hedonism." We're not willing to endure difficult circumstances; we're taught "If it feels good, do it." And we learn the opposite as well—"If it doesn't feel good, get out of the situation." It doesn't matter to restless men and women that their children will be ruined for life; it matters less that they are violating God's laws.

In 1947 Ferdinand Lundberg and Marynia Farnham wrote that divorce is an index of unhappiness in our culture. They stated, "Right now [in 1947] somewhat more than one in every five persons who get married will get divorced. . . . Since 1870 the rate of divorce has increased by leaps and bounds, and statisticians in 1890 worked out a curve that has predicted the rate for each year with fair accuracy. The curve, however, was too conservative; the divorce rate steadily exceeds it because it has been compounding at a rate of 3 percent annually, like money in the bank. By 1965, or in twenty years, if this ascending curve holds up as well as it has since 1890, precisely half of all marriages will be dissolved in divorce."[12]

The statisticians in 1890 were right. In 1978 there were 2.2 million marriages and 1.1 million divorces. According to the Bureau of the Census, the number of children involved in divorces *tripled* in two decades, from 361,000 in 1956 to 1,117,000 in 1976.[13]

But the big question facing all of us is why. Why has divorce skyrocketed, and how is it threatening our civilization? I think there are at least four interrelated reasons.

1. We have forsaken God. In denying the existence of our loving heavenly Father, we have abandoned absolute morality. If we deny the reality of God, we also deny the existence of the absolute moral principles that guide our lives. Harold O.J. Brown, former associate editor of *Christianity Today*, writes that the "current

repudiation of the family in our society is a result of the repudiation of the laws of a created universe."[14] The Playboy philosophers, the humanists, and feminists have taught us via the media that values are relative to the situation we're in. Any woman desiring to have "serial" marriages—to be married ten or twenty times during different "seasons" of her life—should be able to without guilt or ridicule. There's no "Sky Pilot" to prohibit you from enjoying yourself.

So millions of men and women drift from one superficial relationship to another—living with one, marrying another, divorcing, never establishing any kind of long-term commitment with another human being.

2. The cult of selfishness. Bookstore shelves are lined with volumes telling us how we can assert ourselves, dominate others, fornicate without feeling guilty, establish legal arrangements for living with someone outside of marriage, and find "happiness" or "self-actualization." Social commentator Christopher Lasch, writing in *The Culture of Narcissism*, has noted that "people today hunger, not for personal salvation . . . but for the feeling, the momentary illusion of personal well-being, health, and psychic security."[15] Far too many Americans are so caught up in "finding themselves" or some illusive "happiness" they don't care about how many lives they may destroy to achieve their goals. Instead of working through their problems in marriage, they split up.

What has happened is that the philosophers of egocentric hedonism have created a new breed of men and women: modern barbarians who have been *decivilized* to the point where they behave like two-year-old toddlers instead of adults. In the socialization process of training children to be responsible adults, most parents with common sense spend years teaching them to be self-controlled, honest, and responsible. The egocentric hedonists are doing their best to reverse this process. They have produced millions of full-grown toddlers, all clamoring to have their own way—to take drugs, fornicate, kill their babies, and drift through life without purpose or meaning.

3. Man has largely forsaken his role as the head of his family. Many men are undergoing the same identity crisis as women. They're not exactly sure where they are supposed to fit into the scheme of things. Is the man to be the provider or co-provider? Is he supposed to discipline the children or let Mom take care of that aspect of home life? In *Our Dance Has Turned to Death*, Carl Wilson says, ". . .The family, with traditional religious roles for men and women in a life-long monogamous marriage relationship, is the abiding natural foundation for social order, happiness, and stability. When that view is abandoned for selfish individualism, the society will collapse and die. I see the initiating cause as being man's distorting his role, which then initiates family decline. I hold that renewal of society must therefore begin with men."[16]

Wilson believes that because men have forsaken their spiritual leadership role in the family, wives and children are suffering deep psychic damage. Much of the restlessness and discontent in married women is brought on by the husband's failure to exert proper authority. When the husband is a weak and ineffective leader, that task invariably falls upon the wife. Many of you know exactly what I'm talking about; you have become frustrated because you feel as if the entire burden of the family is on your shoulders. Many divorces result because the husband does not understand—or is *unwilling*—to assume his leadership position.

Until the American man makes a conscious decision to take the position as head of his family—and to value his family more than he does his job—I believe we will continue to see an increasing number of divorces and, as a result of these breakups, skyrocketing social problems.

4. War is being waged against the family by the humanists and feminists. This warfare is being carried

out through our communications media. Women are being assaulted in a media blitz to reject their role as mother and homemaker—to be "liberated" to join the work force. The extent of this assault was obvious in November 1981 when no less than thirty-three magazines used their November issues to push for the passage of the Equal Rights Amendment.[17] Thirty-three "women's" magazines were speaking with one voice *against* the traditional American homemaker. Connie Marshner, editor of the *Family Protection Report*, has noted, ". . .There are women's magazines which seem specially written to teach dissatisfaction with one's job. These are the same magazines which assume their readers are ideological feminists—and if the reader is not one when she picks up the magazine, she will be by the time she finishes it, if the editors have their way. Feeding the discontent of women seems a great way to make it big in publishing. But then, feeding improper tastes in men has made Hugh Hefner rich, too."[18]

Feeding the real or imagined discontent of American homemakers will not bring positive solutions. Women who continually read these antifamily magazines will eventually be tempted to discard their husbands and children or become totally restless and discontent in their roles as wives and mothers.

CHILDREN OF DIVORCE

The greatest tragedy in a marriage breakup is what it does to the children. They are the primary victims—the ones who tend to suffer all through their lives because of the selfishness of their parents. Journalist Linda Bird Francke has written *Growing Up Divorced* and several magazine articles dealing with the long-lasting damage done to children who are caught between warring parents. Children between the ages of six and twelve are particularly vulnerable to permanent psychological damage. As she noted, "Children of these ages will experience a gamut of emotions, including anger, fear, and betrayal. But the most persistent reaction is an almost crippling sadness, which permeates every aspect of their behavior and manifests itself in several different ways."[19] These children feel a deep longing that goes unfulfilled; they avoid their real feelings; they feel deprived; they feel a sense of panic as their security is threatened.

Researchers have discovered that boys are more likely than girls to have emotional problems as a result of divorce. "No area of a boy's life seems immune from divorce fallout. Academically, for example, the National Association of Elementary School Principals found that boys from single-parent families have lower achievement ratings than boys from intact families or girls from either family situation. They also suffer deep depressions and experience frequent nightmares. Research shows the list of divorce-related problems for teenagers can run from an increase in drug and alcohol use to feelings of shame and condemnation over the actions of their parents. While adolescent girls may become sexually precocious and even promiscuous following divorce, boys can become sexually insecure and threatened."[20]

The child of divorce, according to psychiatrist Richard A. Gardner, "is very upset because his home life is disintegrating. He is depressed and fearful that he may not see the departing parent, he's exposed to their animosity and he may be being used as a weapon within a loyalty conflict in which he is used by one parent as a spy against the other."[21]

Children victimized by divorce are filled with anger that they've been betrayed and discarded. They often express their rage at society as a whole, as we've seen in the backgrounds of major leaders of the feminist movement. These children themselves are damaged, and they also pose a very real threat to our culture.

Affirming this view is Dr. Armand Nicholi, who testified before the House Select Committee on Children, Youth, and Families on April 25, 1983. He told the committee, "What can we expect if the divorce rate continues to soar? First of all, the quality of family life will continue to deteriorate, producing a society with a higher incidence of mental illness than ever before known. Ninety-five percent of our hospital beds may be taken up by mentally ill patients. The nature of this illness will be characterized primarily by lack of impulse control. In this impulse-ridden society of tomorrow we can expect the assassination of people in authority to be an everyday occurrence. All crimes of violence will increase, even those within the family. Because battered children—if they survive—tend to become parents who in turn abuse their children, the amount of violence within the family will increase exponentially. Aggression turned inward will also increase and the suicide rate will continue to soar."[22]

We will have a situation similar to what happened in Russia following the Soviet experiment in encouraging easy divorce. Children were simply discarded. Dr. Genevieve De Hoyos has written that Russian newspapers in 1935 "gave vent to their indignation at the senseless cruelty and wanton destruction practiced by gangs of youth throughout the Soviet Union. These gangs invaded individual homes, destroying everything they could not take away, and killing mercilessly anyone who resisted them. On trains they molested passengers, sang obscene songs, and prevented them from getting off at their station. Occasionally schools were besieged by these neglected children, who attacked women and beat up children. Gangs were also engaged in regular and violent fights one against the other."[23]

This kind of ultraviolence is what is facing this nation because we have rejected Christian moral principles. Our Lord gives specific moral instructions in the Bible because He knows that since the fall of Adam, man is basically sinful. He wants to protect us from harm by showing how we can live peaceful, productive, and happy lives. The tragedies facing our nation have come because we have rebelled against God; we've been led astray by the preachings of men and women who hate God. By encouraging easy divorce and a life of promiscuity, we are creating a generation of angry, emotionally disturbed children—children who will rise up and take their revenge on all mankind.

TEENAGE SUICIDES

Some of these angry, love-starved children self-destruct rather than face a life without the support of loving parents. Psychiatrist Mary Giffin has spent forty years dealing with troubled youngsters. She recently published a book, *A Cry for Help,* dealing with youth suicides. In an interview in *People* magazine she remarked, "Life for the average teen-ager is becoming more impersonal, aimless, and lonely. Many parents, preoccupied with their own lives, seem to push their children to grow up, to become mini-adults. Children need nurturing and love and they'll kill—themselves— to get it."[24]

When Dr. Giffin was asked how we can stop teen suicides, she replied, "We need better communication between parent and child. In a startingly high proportion of suicides there has been a problem in the parent/child relationship from the beginning—literally. The mother and child never developed a sense of attachment and trust. The manner in which a mother communicates with her baby—the nurturing, breastfeeding, holding—sets the tone of interaction that will go on for the rest of their lives."[25]

Teenage suicides are at epidemic proportions in our society. The death rate among youths aged fifteen to nineteen has increased 200 percent in the past twenty years.[26] More than five thousand youths kill themselves each year, and experts say there are at least *two-to-three* suicides for every one recorded. According to the

National Center for Health Statistics, the suicide trend for children under ten is also increasing.[27]

In *Editorial Research Reports,* Jean Rosenblatt writes, "Suicide claims the lives of four times as many boys and young men as it does girls and young women. And the suicide rate among young whites of either sex is consistently higher than among blacks, although there is some evidence that the gap has narrowed a bit."[28] Citing the typical characteristics of a teenage suicide victim, Mrs. Rosenblatt notes that "two-thirds of the suicidal young people are on poor terms with their families, and that 90 percent feel that their parents do not understand them. Suicidal young people may have experienced child abuse, had an alcoholic parent, or have come from a family where a parent suffered from depression or suicide had occurred. Some seem to be ambivalent about growing up because they equate independence with loss of parental love. These young people are more likely than others to be devastated by loss of any kind."[29]

Note Mrs. Rosenblatt's next statement: "Many see the breakdown in the nuclear family—manifested by soaring divorce rates, more children living in single-parent families and child abuse—as leading to emotional isolation, a key factor in youth suicide. Deprivation of love is a common theme in the lives of suicidal children and young people. Young children who are ignored, not touched, or made to feel unwanted may eventually respond by taking their own life."[30]

Teen suicides, youth violence and crime, emotional illness—these are the results of the breakup of the nuclear family. They are the inevitable results of men and women refusing to work out their problems in a marriage relationship. By "doing their own thing," millions of irresponsible husbands and wives are literally condemning their children to death or to lives as emotional cripples.

Dr. Harold Voth warns, "Deprive the child of a happy

home life and you deprive him of his mental health. If current trends which are eroding the family continue—and those social movements which downgrade the expression of a woman's femininity within a family are prominent among the eroding forces—society as we know it now will end. A strong society comprises strong men and women. Strong individuals come from only one place—from solid families."[31]

ILLEGITIMATE AND DISPOSABLE CHILDREN

One of the most frightening new phenomena facing our society is the growing number of mothers who choose to desert their children. On a secular talk show recently, I was opposite a feminist who had chosen to abandon her children to the custody of the father. She declared that the children would interfere with the social life she wanted to pursue.

Until recently it was normal for courts to award custody of a child to the mother in a divorce action. In 90 percent of the divorce cases, the child went with the mother. Now judges are tending toward so-called joint custody of the child or increasingly are giving the father custody. Many mothers are willingly giving up their children. Statistics show that at least 565,000 mothers now live apart from their children—more than double the figure for 1970.[32]

One of these mothers is Patricia Fontes of Santa Ana, California. She says she tried to be a mother for fifteen years, but just couldn't cope with it any longer. "I needed to find out who I was—and what I was doing with my life," she said. So in 1980 she deserted her three children and husband and moved into her own apartment "to find herself."[33]

The trend away from awarding custody to the mother is the result of feminist agitation. Prior to the push for "nonsexist" laws, judges usually awarded custody to the mother under the "doctrine of tender years," presuming that the children were better off with the mother unless she was unfit. Dr. Peter B. Dunn, clinical assistant professor at Downstate Medical Center in New York, observes, "One might want it to be true that it doesn't really matter which is the absent parent, but young children have feelings about their mother that overwhelm those about their fathers."[34]

UNWED MOTHERS

Another major social problem facing our country because of the sexual revolution is the growing number of unwed mothers. Right now at least 17 percent of all children in America are illegitimate. Statistics indicate that in 1979, for example, 597,000 illegitimate babies were born—up 50 percent since 1970. According to political columnist Allan Brownfeld, "Nearly a third of the babies born to white teen-agers and 83 percent born to black teen-agers were illegitimate."[35] Black families are being especially hard hit—in 1979, 50 percent of all black children born in America were born out of wedlock. Brownfeld says, "Part of the reason for this trend is that more and more young people have been largely abandoned by their parents."[36]

When these teenagers feel unloved at home, they seek love elsewhere. Often they simply run away and end up on the streets selling their bodies; others find a lover, get pregnant, and go on Aid to Dependent Children. They get pregnant just to get out of their homes.

According to the most recent statistics available, more than 666,000 children were born out of wedlock—more than four times as many as the 142,000 illegitimate children born in 1950.[37] Eleanor Holmes Norton, former head of the Equal Employment Opportunity Commission, laments this condition by asking the question, "What kind of fresh start can there be for us when half the next generation will consist of children who were raised by children?"[38]

CAREER WOMEN AND FAMILY LIFE

In a survey taken by the Public Agenda Foundation, 848 workers were asked a variety of questions dealing with the working woman and her family life. Of those surveyed, 56 percent of the men and 43 percent of the women believe that a woman who wants to work should not have children. "And 63 percent of the men and 52 percent of the women think that being a working mother is bad for very young children. However, 90 percent of those surveyed agreed that most working mothers need the money, and a solid majority believe day-care centers need to be improved."[39]

Another survey was conducted in 1982 by the Free Congress/Sindlinger polling organization. They discovered that 63.6 percent of the women were working partly because of financial need, partly for fulfillment. Among these working women, 45.7 percent said they didn't feel their children were being hurt by working.[40]

Another survey conducted by Louis Harris and Associates for General Mills discovered that 39 percent of those women surveyed would prefer to work at home; 14 percent prefer to do only volunteer work, making a total of 53 percent who do not want to be in the labor force at all. Another 32 percent wanted only part-time work, leaving 12 percent who wanted full-time employment outside the home.[41] But the economic realities of the times we live in often make it essential that women work.

Yet many women find it difficult to compete in a man's work world. Alexandra Symonds, a feminist psychoanalyst, has dealt with numerous career women—women who can't cope with their submissive natures and the demands of the work world. She attributes their emotional problems to what she calls "the psychology of submission," which, she says, has kept women from becoming "autonomous." The women she has dealt with are dependent on others and have a fear of being alone.

"To be alone," Symonds says, "is to experience an unbearable void. Since they do not experience their identity except in terms of others, they feel at their best when taking care of a husband or child. They focus almost exclusively on externals and others."[42]

Symonds claims that the dependency women feel comes from their cultural conditioning, not from any innate character traits common to all women. She believes this dependency is a neurotic behavior pattern that must be broken if women are to be truly "liberated." She has dealt with women "who seem to get very little satisfaction from their achievements because they feel a failure unless they have a man, yet their outer manner of success and self-sufficiency invariably attracts men who are trying to avoid excessively dependent women."[43]

Dr. Harold Voth has also dealt extensively with career women, and his conclusions are diametrically opposed to those of feminist Symonds. He observes about women, "Their natural instinct was pushing them toward heterosexuality, marriage, motherhood; something else within them was pushing them toward the continuance of their vocation or career. I believe this inner conflict accounts for the high suicide rate in professional women who are still in the childbearing age range (much higher than in men or the general population)."[44]

Many feminists in their thirties who have pursued careers have grown tired of struggling in the business world. They are experiencing "baby hunger"—that innate, God-given desire within every normal woman to give birth to a child.

Dr. Voth warns career women to take the long view of life: what will they be doing in ten, twenty, or thirty years if they refuse to marry? He cautions, "The woman who embarks on a vocational career must be aware that a significant aspect of her basic nature will go unsatisfied if she never has a family. She should be aware of what she is getting into as she sets her life course."[45]

Women who try to mix a professional career *with a family* also have difficulties. Trying to juggle a profession, the responsibilities of caring for children, and taking care of a house is simply too much for many women. Because few are capable of being "super-moms," the breakup of the family is almost inevitable. A survey reported in *Glamour* magazine shows that among women who earn $50,000 or more a year, the divorce rate is *four times the national average.*

Another survey indicates that women who earn $25,000 or more a year are twice as likely to be divorced as women in the general population. Among professional women whose median income is between $40–50,000 a year, 46 percent are single, 19 percent are divorced or separated, and 58 percent are childless. Women who go through graduate school are more likely to divorce than women who receive only undergraduate degrees.[46]

SUMMARY

The "women's liberation" movement has given birth to some ugly social problems—problems that threaten the survival of our nation. When a man does not fulfill his proper role within the family and when a woman casts off her vital role as the nurturer of children, the basic unit of society begins to disintegrate. The results are the murder of unborn babies, rampant venereal diseases, teenage pregnancies, teenage suicides, a skyrocketing divorce rate, mental illness, street crime, runaway children, and many other social problems.

The next chapter discusses the importance of the family unit and how the restless woman responds to God in modern culture. If restless women understood how important they are in preserving our society, they would be far more satisfied with their roles as wives, mothers, and homemakers. They would not suffer from a lack of self-esteem, nor would they fall victim to feminist and humanist propaganda. They would be far happier and content if they had an intimate relationship with Jesus Christ.

NOTES

[1] George Leonard, "The End of Sex," *Reader's Digest* (March 1983):132.

[2] Ibid., 132–133.

[3] Peter Marin, "A Revolution's Broken Promises," *Psychology Today* (July 1983):53–54.

[4] "Swingers' Questionable Mental Health," *Psychology Today* (February 1983):70.

[5] Carl W. Wilson, *Our Dance Has Turned to Death* (Tyndale House, 1981), 75.

[6] "The Status of Children, Youth, and Families, '79" (Washington: U.S. Department of Health and Human Services).

[7] John Leo, "Herpes Scourge of the Sexual Revolution," *Reader's Digest* (January 1983):128.

[8] *"Herpes—Just the Facts"* (Washington: Eagle Forum Education & Legal Defense Fund).

[9] Steven Findlay, "New Sexual Diseases Add to AIDS, Herpes Furor," *U.S.A. Today* (June 14, 1983):6D.

[10] Ibid.

[11] *"Herpes—Just the Facts."*

[12] Ferdinand Lundberg and Marynia F. Farnham, *Modern Woman— The Lost Sex* (New York: Harper Brothers, 1947), 37–38.

[13] "Divorce, Child Custody and Child Support" (Washington: U.S. Department of Commerce, Bureau of the Census), Series P-23, No. 84 (June 1979).

[14] *The Capsule* (July-August 1980):4.

[15] Onalee McGraw, *The Family, Feminism and the Therapeutic State* (Washington: Heritage Foundation, 1980), 27.

[16] Wilson, *Our Dance Has Turned to Death*, xv.

[17] "Militant Feminists Demand Restructuring of Family Values," *Conservative Digest* (May 1982):16.

18 Connaught C. Marshner, *The New Traditional Woman* (Washington: Free Congress Research and Education Foundation, 1982), 3.

19 Linda Bird Francke, "Children of Divorce," *Family Circle* (July 12, 1983):79.

20 Linda Bird Francke, "Sons and Daughters of Divorce," *Santa Ana Register* (June 12, 1983): K5.

21 Frank Green, "Children Become Rebellious Victims in Divorce Rows," *San Diego Union* (December 28, 1982):1.

22 "House Families Committee Hears Harvard Prof. Condemn Divorce," *Family Protection Report* (May 1983):1.

23 Genevieve De Hoyos, *Feminism or Familism?* (Provo, Utah, Northbridge, 1978), 23.

24 "A Double Suicide Adds to the National Tragedy of Teenagers Who Take Their Own Lives," *People* (June 27, 1983):33.

25 Ibid., 34.

26 Ibid., 33.

27 Jean Rosenblatt, "Youth Suicide," *Editorial Research Reports* (June 12, 1981):431.

28 Ibid., 432.

29 Ibid., 433–34.

30 Ibid., 436.

31 Harold M. Voth, *The Castrated Family* (Kansas City, Mo.: Universal Press Syndicate, 1977), 207.

32 Christine Doudna, "Mothers Who Give Up Their Children: The List Grows," *San Diego Union* (October 31, 1982):D4.

33 Ibid.

34 Ibid.

35 Allan Brownfeld, "Family Unit Threatened by Rising Illegitimacy," *Washington Times* (September 28, 1981).

36 Ibid.

37 Sheila Caudle, "Poverty Haunts USA's Children," *USA Today* (June 10, 1983):8A.

38 Brownfeld, "Family Unit Threatened by Rising Illegitimacy."

39 "Moms, Jobs Don't Mix, Say Many Workers," *USA Today* (July 26, 1983):1D.

40 *Family Protection Report* (March 1982):4.

41 *The Phyllis Schlafly Report* (December 1982):2.

42 Alexandra Symonds, "The Liberated Woman: Healthy and Neurotic," *American Journal of Psychoanalysis* (Fall 1974):180.

[43] Alexandra Symonds, "Neurotic Dependency in Successful Women," *Journal of the American Academy of Psychoanalysis*, vol. 4, no. 1 (1976):101.

[44] Voth, *The Castrated Family*, 195.

[45] Ibid., 196

[46] *The Phyllis Schlafly Report* (December 1982):2.

7.

The Untold Story
of Women

The restless woman has been caught in the middle of a political and religious battleground not of her making. On one side are the feminists, agitating for "our rights" and demanding radical social change in every dimension of our lives; on the other side are the forces of traditionalism led by women who believe in the biblical standards for morality and successful living. And the restless woman has no spiritual or ideological weapons with which to fight the battle.

This defenseless person has probably been brought up in a traditional American family and feels she must cling to her middle-class values, but she's in continual emotional turmoil. Feminist magazines assail her with thoughts of an exciting life outside of the home; the traditionalists tell her she has important responsibilities she must fulfill *within* the home. Her dilemma is deciding who's right.

How has all this affected her belief in God? I believe that women have a natural tendency to seek spiritual truth. Unchurched women often look in the wrong places, but they still are more likely to seek supernatural guidance than men are. The frequency with which horoscope columns appear in women's magazines shows that women instinctively desire spiritual or supernatural leading. Women are more likely to consult with mediums or become ensnared in witchcraft than men are.

Men are generally not as spiritually attuned as women or as inclined to spiritual matters. I think God has given females a spiritual sensitivity—a special gift of discernment or "women's intuition" that leads us to seek spiritual truth. Part of this tendency, I think, is our natural inclination toward dependency, whether focused on our husbands or on the Lord. Men are naturally aggressive and self-sufficient and therefore may have a harder time coming to the Lord or expressing dependency.

A DISTORTED PICTURE

I think the mass media often present a distorted picture of the true desires and concerns of women. Normally television and newspapers highlight the armies of feminists marching for their rights; we rarely see the armies of women volunteers working at the Red Cross, visiting nursing homes, or ministering to prisoners. Television documentaries showing woman missionaries working among primitive tribes around the world or women sharing the gospel of Jesus Christ with prostitutes on the streets of Los Angeles are nonexistent. The media seldom talk about the thousands of homes for pregnant teenagers provided to give them an alternative to abortion. The media often fail to mention the concerns and victories that moral-minded, family-oriented, Christian women are achieving across the nation.

The humanist-controlled press will never acknowledge the women who are spending their lives helping others in need. Nor will the humanist press tell the story of how politically active, conservative women are working to preserve the American family.

One would never know from reading newspapers or watching television that America is moving toward a spiritual revival. This truth became evident to researchers conducting an extensive opinion poll for the Connecticut Mutual Life Insurance Company in 1981. The poll revealed that religious belief among Americans is becoming more important than any other factor in determining behavior. According to these researchers, "The impact of religion on our social and political institutions may be only the beginning of a trend that could change the face of America." The researchers conclude, "Moral issues through religion have vaulted to the forefront of the political dialogue. Something unusual is happening."[1]

A Gallup Poll taken several years ago disclosed that 94 percent of Americans today "believe in God or a universal spirit"; 71 percent believe in a life after death. According to Burton Yale Pines in *Back to Basics*, "In surveys conducted in 1978 and 1979, for example, Gallup found that more than 80 percent of Americans believe that Christ is divine, a like number believe in the Resurrection, more than one-third of the adult population has had a 'life-changing religious experience' (a phenomenon broadly known as being 'born again'), two-thirds believe that God 'rewards and punishes,' half believe that God started the human race by creating Adam and Eve, 42 percent of parents say grace before meals with their children and nearly one-third of parents pray or meditate with their children."[2]

Another Gallup survey reported that 62 percent of today's "evangelical Christians" are women.[3] This really shouldn't surprise us. Women have always outnumbered men in America's churches.

Indeed, the Connecticut Mutual study found that "women are more inclined than men to be highly religious (34 percent to 19 percent)."[4] In addition, "Our findings suggest that the increasing impact of religion on our social and political institutions may be only the beginning of a trend that could change the face of America.[5]

The researchers also noted, "This report identifies a cohesive and powerful group of Americans, approximately 45 million strong, as 'intensely religious,' and demonstrates that religious Americans are likely to vote often and to become highly involved in their local communities."[6]

I am certain that a majority of that 45 million are women—women committed to God and to moral principles.

WOMEN IN AMERICAN HISTORY

Godly women have filled an important role in American history. The proportion of women actively involved in church work has almost always outnumbered men. For example, "female church members had vastly outnumbered males during most of the colonial period. Even during revivals, which were particularly effective in recruiting male converts, men had not always equaled the number of women joining. During the First Great Awakening (1739–1743), for example, the proportion of women admitted to Connecticut churches averaged about 56 percent."[7]

Women took leadership roles in organizing missionary societies to share the gospel overseas. According to historian Rosemary Skinner Keller, "More females became involved in women's missionary society work after the Civil War than in all areas of the social reform and woman's rights movements combined. Between 1861 and 1894, foreign missionary societies were organized by and for women in thirty-three denominations, and home missionary societies in seventeen."[8]

Christian women were actively involved in social reform as well. Margaret Barrett Allen Prior was the first missionary for the New York Female Moral Reform Society. She spent fifteen years of her life working among the poor in New York slums and helping to deliver prostitutes from their way of life.[9]

Eliza Stewart led a crusade against alcohol abuse.

Frances Willard was the moving force behind the Woman's Christian Temperance Union. When she was elected president of the WCTU in 1879, she broadened the concerns of the organization beyond alcoholism to other social problems. Under her brilliant leadership the WCTU crusaded for women's suffrage, better schools, labor reform, prison reform, urban welfare, help for prostitutes, and an end to the use of narcotics.[10] She understood the vital link between Christian beliefs and action. Her strong Christian convictions were translated into specific reforms aimed at uplifting the lot of mankind, not only in the United States, but around the world.

Frances Willard's major concern was the preservation of the American family. All the social problems she dealt with threatened the safety of the home. She was determined to protect and defend the institution of marriage from any outside forces.

In her autobiography, *Glimpses of Fifty Years: The Autobiography of an American Woman,* Frances Willard writes, "With all its faults, and they are many, I believe the present marriage system to be the greatest triumph of Christianity, and that it has created and conserves more happy homes than the world has ever before known. Any law that renders less binding the mutual, life-long loyalty of one man and one woman to each other, which is the central idea of every home, is an unmitigated curse to that man and woman, to that home, and to humanity."[11]

Frances Willard did not spend a lifetime demanding "her rights." She was not motivated by hatred, but by compassion. She saw men and women suffering the effects of alcohol and drug abuse, of prostitution and oppression. She determined to rectify the injustices she saw in her society. Her motives were not selfish, but were directed toward bettering the lives of all men and women.

Another zealous Christian woman of the nineteenth

century was Catherine Beecher, who spent her life crusading for educational reforms. She established training institutes to educate young women in home-making and the arts, believing that women had a special role to fulfill as mothers and wives.

By educating young women in the science of what later came to be known as "home economics," Catherine Beecher felt they would be greater assets to their husbands and children. In her view, God had given women the responsibility of training children in right-eousness. Her view was only partially correct: both the father and mother are to train up their children. Through her voluminous writings Catherine Beecher became the most famous spokeswoman for the "tradi-tionalist" cause during the nineteenth century.

These Christian women, and many others in our history, were not "trapped housewives" by any means. They were intelligent, dedicated, and hardworking. They exemplified the ideal picture of womanhood as shown in Proverbs 31. They were keepers of the home as well as active in their community. Their purpose in life was not to satisfy their own desires, but to minister healing, love, and hope to those less fortunate. They were selflessly devoted to their particular causes—flwhether pulling young women out of prostitution, helping to establish mental asylums for women, or crusading against alcohol. They were not devoting their lives to the elusive goal of "self-fulfillment" or "hap-piness." They *were* fulfilled and happy—but this came as a byproduct of their willingness to give of them-selves.

One result of the work and influence of these godly women is that the crime rate in America declined for nearly a century. It was during the 1830s and 1840s that American cities began to experience terrible crime problems. Alarmed by this epidemic of crime and the high rate of alcohol consumption (ten gallons per person per year in 1829), churches set about to remedy the situation. One solution was found in promoting "character education" in schools and in the print media. In books, newspapers, and magazines, readers were taught the value of honesty, industriousness, sobriety, and self-control.

According to political commentator Reo M. Christenson, about one-third of the articles in *Ladies Home Journal, The Woman's Home Companion,* and *Good Housekeeping* from 1890 to 1910 dealt with the importance of child rearing, character development, and the mother's character in molding the future leaders of the nation.

At the turn of the century, Edward Bok was editor of *The Ladies Home Journal.* Bok also served as an editor of a unique, ten-volume set of inspirational books designed for children and young adults. *The Library of Inspiration and Achievement* was filled with articles expressing morality, honesty, thrift, and heroism. Its purpose was to instill sound Christian principles in youth.

In one essay Bok told his young readers, "There is no influence to be compared with that of a good woman over the life of a young man. It means everything to him, his success in every phase of life. Men are by nature coarse and brutal; it is the influence of woman which softens them. But no influence is productive of the best and surest results unless we make ourselves susceptible to it. If we lack faith in woman, if we fail in the right ideal of womanhood, all her influence will be as naught upon us. . . . Man's best friend is the woman who loves him. That should be the faith of every young man toward woman; that should be his absolute conviction, and he should show it by an attitude of respect and deference toward her."[12]

It was through character education in books, women's magazines, and *McGuffey's Reader's* that America's crime rate declined for nearly a hundred years. Only during the 1920s—an age of rebellion—did the crime rate begin to rise again.

WOMEN'S MOVEMENTS TODAY

This same kind of morality movement is taking place in America today. There are hundreds of thousands of women involved in organizations such as Eagle Forum and Concerned Women for America. These are women who know who they are. They are confident of their worth; they see the social decline taking place in America and they're actively involved in trying to stop it. For example, the committed women of Concerned Women for America are working in churches and neighborhoods to build a network of Christian women for prayer and action. Their concerns are "protecting the rights of the family," rather than their personal rights. They are not concerned about "self-fulfillment" or chasing some nebulous ideal of "happiness." They are seeking to preserve the nuclear family and society from destruction.

While these women are working to preserve traditional values, there are other women in the church seeking to usurp power. "Christian feminists" such as Letha Scanzoni and Nancy Hardesty, authors of *All We're Meant to Be*, are challenging not simply church hierarchy, but the validity of Scripture itself in making their feminist demands. One author notes that feminists "occupy center stage in current discussions of women in the church because they often comprise the most articulate, well-organized and politically minded of church women and because many denominational leaders, having experienced a certain measure of guilt because of their past stance toward women, are eager to redress grievances quickly. Yet, even the most ardent of their supporters will admit that the feminists wield an influence that is out of proportion to their numbers in the churches and that introduces viewpoints from outside denominational traditions."[13]

I believe that one of the greatest dangers facing the Christian church today is women who advocate feminist viewpoints. As I travel across the United States and speak with thousands of Christian women, it appears that lines are being drawn between the traditionalists in the church and women who are leaning toward the feminist positions. Many times this division occurs gradually and unknowingly as women begin to drift away from the absolutes in the Word of God. The differences at first may be minimal, but the division widens as the emphasis shifts to more of self and less of God.

This trend is occurring even in traditionally conservative, fundamentalist churches, but it has been more widespread in the mainline denominations. It grieves me to think that a root of bitterness is growing in our churches because of feminism. I caution "Christian feminists" against causing divisions in the church. If they have legitimate grievances, they should state their position—once—and commit it to the Lord. Anything more than that is rebellion.

A philosophy based on selfishness, rebellion, and anger should have absolutely no place in our churches. Feminists should not be allowed to infect Christian women with their alien ideologies, which are based in large measure on Marxist and humanist teachings.

Fortunately feminists constitute a minority both in the church and in society. Yet they wield considerable power in attempting to mold public opinion. Opinion polls indicate, however, that most American women—whether restless or content—have not accepted the feminist philosophy. Feminists have won victories because they have been able to influence government leaders, whose moral viewpoints often differ from the general populace. The Connecticut Mutual report notes, "The gap between the public and its leaders is to some extent a moral gap. We find that across the entire range of moral issues, leaders are consistently more liberal in their judgments."[14] Only 42 percent of the leaders, for example, think that homosexuality is morally wrong, compared with 71 percent of the general public; only 36 percent of the leaders think abortion is wrong, compared with 65 percent of the public.[15]

Although the feminist philosophy—based as it is on an anti-God premise—has affected the thinking of scores of women, I do not believe it has converted very many restless women into confirmed atheists. It has affected their relationships with their husbands and children, however, and has directly impaired the proper functioning of the family according to God's pattern.

NOTES

[1]*The Connecticut Mutual Life Report on American Values in the '80s: The Impact of Belief* (Connecticut Mutual Life Insurance Co., 1981), 9.

[2]Burton Yale Pines, *Back to Basics* (New York: William Morrow, 1982), 184–85.

[3]Ibid., 191.

[4]*Connecticut Mutual Life Report*, 19.

[5]Ibid., 7.

[6]Ibid.

[7]*The Nineteenth Century, a Documentary History*, vol. 1, Women and Religion in America (San Francisco: Harper & Row, 1981), 2.

[8]Ibid., 242.

[9]Ibid., 300–301.

[10]Ibid., 322.

[11]Frances Willard, *Glimpses of Fifty Years: The Autobiography of an American Woman* (Chicago: H. J. Smith & Co., 1889), 611.

[12]Edward W. Bok, ed., *Success and How to Win It* (New York: The University Society, 1902), 318.

[13]Janet Wilson James, ed., *Women in American Religion* (Philadelphia: Univ. of Pennsylvania Press, 1978), 190.

[14]*Connecticut Mutual Life Report*, 27–28.

[15]Ibid., 28.

8.

The New Traditional Woman

Caught in the middle of a feminist/traditionalist battle-ground, the restless woman must make a choice. She can join the feminists and spend her life with the family agitators who would destroy the "patriarchal" system; or she can join those who are working to preserve Christian morality and the traditional family. From all indications, both within and without the movement, it appears that many feminists are finally coming to grips with the reality of human nature.

As some of these activists pass thirty years of age, they find themselves agonizing over whether or not they should have babies. As my husband, Tim, mentions in his book *The Battle for the Family*, hardline feminist Phyllis Chesler finally felt she needed to have a child—even though she had no husband. She knew she was going to be rebuffed by her allies in the feminist movement when she said, "The unique intimacy and transcendence offered in the birth of a child was something I didn't want to deny myself."[1]

Betty Friedan discovered that many other hardline feminists have grown weary and disillusioned with waging war against the family and for "equal rights." She candidly admits their disillusionment in her book *The Second Stage.* Her once-enthusiastic allies were defecting. They were coming to their senses. Many were realizing that it might not be so bad to get married, have babies, a loving dependence on a husband, and live a peaceful life in suburbia. A number of women once involved in the feminist movement are finally able to see where the movement is leading them: to a life of misery, anger, loneliness, and death.

I believe we are seeing a return to basic morality in America.

In an article published in the Concerned Women for America newsletter in January 1984, I stated how ex-feminists are finding the truth. "There seems to be an increasing number of women who are taking the time to re-evaluate the direction the feminist/humanist philosophy is leading them. They are either losing interest or are making a deliberate turn-around in their attitudes regarding family, God and country. It's a very encouraging sign to me!

"Our Washington, D.C., lobbyist, Barbara Gibbons, is a prime example of a feminist who had made a 180-degree change in her life since she became a Christian just a few years ago.

"Another former feminist met me after a speaking engagement not long ago and related how her whole life had been spent fighting for the ERA [Equal Rights Amendment]—joining in marches and conferences—and being an 'activist' in NOW. After having her eyes opened to the harm the ERA would cause her family, she became totally disinterested in the movement and committed herself to wholeheartedly supporting anti-feminist causes.

"I also received a letter recently from a woman who had been influenced by Jane Fonda. She recounted the sad story of her life. She had voted for the radical Peace and Freedom Party, picketed with feminists, and smoked marijuana—all in the name of sexual liberation. Following the feminist ideals of 'womanhood,' she had developed a serious drinking problem, deserted her husband, undergone several abortions, and is now sterile as a result of her 'sexual freedom.'

"Fortunately, her story does not end with this string of personal tragedies. In her desperation and despair, she cried out to the Lord for help and He heard her prayers! She told me that she's now a committed Christian who is voting as a patriotic American and is absolutely opposed to the ERA and to the goals of the feminist movement.

"She also said that many of the feminists she had met were lesbians, anti-family, anti-God, and pro-humanist. In trying to be a liberated female, she said, she became only 'alienated not liberated.'

"When the humanist and feminist philosophies are exposed for what they really are, there are those women who will become disenchanted with the false promises and deceit. These former feminists I've just mentioned are among a growing number of such women.

"Only by living according to God's Word can a woman become truly liberated. Unfortunately, these women have been deceived and made captives of godless philosophies. In this regard, Paul has a stern warning for us in Colossians 2:8: 'See to it that no one takes you captive through hollow and deceptive philosophy, which depends on human tradition and the basic principles of this world rather than on Christ.' As a result of their deception, these feminists are miserable, angry people. The only possible way they will ever find any kind of contentment is to turn away from their vain, godless philosophies and embrace the Son of God. Only then will they have true 'peace and freedom.' "[2]

In his book *Back to Basics*, Burton Yale Pines notes the growing traditionalist movement. "No longer does the feminist movement by itself set the agenda for debate on women's issues. No longer is this movement the voice which policy-makers hear speaking for all American women. Shattering this onetime feminist monopoly are women who previously were content to remain in their kitchens and care for their families and who defined 'activism' as attending PTA meetings and baking for church bazaars."[3]

Political analyst Connie Marshner has given a name to this new kind of woman who is actively involved in preserving Christian principles. She calls her the "new traditional woman." She is new in the sense that she's a modern woman; she's traditional because she realizes that there are certain moral principles and social institutions that *must* be preserved if we are to have any kind of orderly, civilized society. The "new traditional woman" realizes that God has created male and female and has given us clear instructions in His Word as to how we are to treat one another. We do not have to flounder with situation ethics or be confused as to what is "right" and what is "wrong." The Bible tells us.

The "new traditional woman," Marshner says, "will transmit civilization and humanity to the 21st century. Make no mistake. It is women who will do it. This involves nothing less than a change of heart by a whole generation. To save our society, we must change our hearts, and change the hearts of our fellow men. If our hearts are changed, our politics will change, and our public policies will change."[4]

We can change our society, depending on the choices we make. I believe all of us—whether restless or content, churched or unchurched—have choices to make about life priorities. We are continually changing, for better or worse. The questions I pose are these: If we are in transition, whether in terms of morality or career goals, where will these changes take us? Where will we be and what will we be doing in five, ten, or fifteen years? If we are adopting new attitudes, will these assure our peace and fulfillment? Will they be in step with God's plan for women? Or will they simply cause us more frustration and heartache?

If you are a restless woman searching for answers, do you sincerely believe that the feminist movement will provide the answers? If you choose to discard "middle-class values" or Christian morality, what will fill the void in your soul? Will it be selfish goals or serving others? Will it contribute to a stronger family or create instability? Will it be Marxism or humanism? Will it be hatred and rebellion? These are things you must seriously consider.

Feminist Judith Bardwick observes in her book *In Transition* that our whole culture is undergoing such rapid changes in basic values and beliefs that our society has become unstable. "Many have been and will continue to be forced, by changes in their values or changes in the values of others, to significantly alter how they behave. Shifts in basic values have created profound dislocations for the large number of people whose lives have become very different from what they expected when they were growing up."[5]

THE RESTLESS WOMAN AS VICTIM

The restless woman has borne the brunt of society's instability. The shifting value systems, the philosophy of "doing your own thing," and the attacks on Christian morality have afflicted women with an uneasiness about their purpose and role.

All of us are in transition—but to where and for what purpose? The feminist movement, Bardwick writes, "is clearest about what it is rejecting from the past. But the movement is not clear about what norms will replace those which have been rejected; new norms are hard to imagine."[6]

That is a frightening statement. The feminists are bent on destroying traditional morality and restructuring our society in their image, but they aren't sure if their new order will work. "Christian feminists" Letha Scanzoni and Nancy Hardesty admit, "The end of male chauvinism will also mean the end of chivalry in the traditional sense of men continually smoothing the way for the 'weaker sex.' Women can no longer expect doors to open, seats to become vacant, packages to be carried for them simply because they're women. Women can no longer rely on tears and manipulation rather than reason and hard work to achieve their ends. But hopefully, courtesy and consideration will be extended to all persons on an equal basis."[7]

Do women really wanted to be treated like men? Do we really want to lose the respect and honor that was once shown to us by them? Do we want to lose romance? I, for one, don't. I enjoy doors being opened for me and seats being offered to me—not because I am weak and unable to do things for myself, but because it is a gesture of respect and dignity offered to the feminine woman. I don't feel demeaned or less than human when a gentleman openly shows his respect for me. Yet all of this will be lost in a "feminist" utopia. We will lose far more than chivalry if the feminists achieve their goals. We will lose love, compassion, gentleness, and warmth in all of our relationships. These have already been lost in many male-female relationships where lust is substituted for love.

To insist that women be treated "equally" with men is to deprive men of a natural need to protect and support. It creates insecurities and fears in them. It creates confusion so that a man does not know how to treat a woman. He's not sure what she expects or what will insult her. A division is created between males and females when they are forced to compete with each other. The relationship between men and women should be one of cooperation, not fierce competition.

The tendency of women to compete in the work world with men results in their masculinization. Few men are attracted to a macho-feminist. A masculine man is attracted by the feminine characteristics in a woman—qualities such as gentleness and virtue. He's not seeking a clone of himself. The attraction that men and women have for each other is in their "differentness"—not their sameness. A man sees temperament traits in a woman that he lacks but desires; the woman sees attributes in a man that she lacks but admires. Within the marriage bond a man and woman find completeness. They become one. Often opposites attract each other in marriage; a man will marry a woman who has strengths where he is weak and vice versa.

Unfortunately many women are being victimized by the feminist movement. They are urged to reject their natural feminine nature that is distinct from masculinity.

Even feminist Judith Bardwick is worried about the ultimate goal of radical feminism. Bardwick sees an androgynous (unisex) society, where all sexual distinctions have been erased. "...The danger of the androgynous vision," she says, "lies in the possibility that our goal will become the development of an asexual culture. While many of the things that we do are essentially asexual in the sense that it does not make any difference whether they are done by a woman or a man, it would be a pity if an emphasis on adrogyny blurred the complementary excitements that are created from the differences in how women and men perceive and feel."[8]

SELFISHNESS VERSUS SELFLESSNESS

Contrasting the feminist world view with the Christian viewpoint, I find a basic thread of selfishness running through all feminist writings. There is an emphasis on "my rights," "my goals," "my body," and "my self-fulfillment." Feminists have openly admitted that the invention of the birth-control pill and the legalization of abortion have been powerful social forces in radicalizing women. The "freedom" to fornicate outside of marriage and to murder their unborn children is looked upon as a great stride forward in the status of women.

This trend toward selfishness is self-destructive rather than liberating. It goes against what I believe is the basic nature of a woman—to think of others before herself. Some feminist psychologists look on "selflessness" as a neurotic behavior, instilled in women by a male chauvinist social system. But I believe God gave the natural tendency toward giving, nurturing, serving, and comforting. To deny this selfless nature is to deny our personalities and the purpose for our existence.

Throughout the Bible we are taught to be more concerned for others than ourselves. *Through the act of giving we find fulfillment and purpose.* God's Word tells us in Philippians 2:3–8: "Do nothing out of selfish ambition or vain conceit, but in humility consider others better than yourselves. Each of you should look not only to your own interests but also to the interest of others. Your attitude should be the same as that of Christ Jesus: Who, being in very nature God, did not consider equality with God something to be grasped, but made himself nothing, taking the very nature of a servant, being made in human likeness. And being found in appearance as a man, he humbled himself and became obedient to death—even death on a cross!"

Whether we are male or female, we are to be concerned about the welfare of others. It is not a sin to take care of our own needs, but we should be willing to give of ourselves to others. Our attitude should be one of humility—the same kind of humility displayed by Jesus Christ when He willingly took on human form and was born in a manger.

In Luke 22:27 Jesus tells His disciples, "I am among you as one who serves." He came into the world, not to rule over us, but to serve us and redeem us from the curse of sin. Jesus should be our model and guide. At one point in His ministry He washed His disciples' feet to show them that they should have the same humility in serving others. If the God of creation was willing to wash feet, shouldn't we be willing to serve others—especially our husbands and children?

How different Jesus' attitude is from that of the world. The world teaches us to fight for our rights; we must strive and claw our way to the top. We must picket, protest, scream, and destroy so we can have our own way. That is the way of the world. What is the fruit of the world's ideology of selfishness? Look around and see the ruined lives among your friends and relatives. There's no one living whose life has not been adversely affected by the selfishness and hatred of someone else. The apostle James reminds us in James 3:16–17, "For where you have envy and selfish ambition, there you find disorder and every evil practice. But the wisdom that comes from heaven is first of all pure; then peace loving, considerate, submissive, full of mercy and good fruit, impartial and sincere."

Are you in transition toward a life of selfishness and self-indulgence or are you seeking opportunities to serve others—to meet the needs of those hurting around you?

NOTES

[1] Tim LaHaye, *The Battle for the Family* (Old Tappan, N.J.: Fleming H. Revell, 1982), 143.

[2] Beverly LaHaye, "Ex-Feminists Are Finding Truth," *CWA Newsletter* (January 1984):4.

[3] Burton Yale Pines, *Back to Basics* (New York: William Morrow, 1982), 157.

[4] Connaught C. Marshner, *The New Traditional Woman* (Washington: Free Congress Research & Education Foundation, 1982), 3.

[5] Judith Bardwick, *In Transition* (New York: Holt, Rinehart & Winston, 1979), 2–3.

[6] Ibid., 21.

[7] Letha Scanzoni and Nancy Hardesty, *All We're Meant to Be* (Waco, Tex.: Word Books, 1975), 207.

[8] Bardwick, *In Transition*, 17.

9.

Some Restlessness Is for Our Good

We all have experienced restlessness in one form or another. Restlessness comes from different sources, sometimes for our good and sometimes for our destruction. Wrong reactions to some forms of restlessness can add to our problems. Nevertheless, God sometimes uses a spirit of restlessness to direct us in finding His will for our lives.

The opposite of restlessness is contentment. Certainly restlessness is more characteristic of human life. Although contentment is uncommon, it is possible to have it momentarily when all circumstances seem right and pleasing.

While Tim and I were on vacation a few years ago, the circumstances seemed near-perfect. We were in a beautiful place conducive to rest and relaxation. The weather was cooperating to make it exactly as we had dreamed. We were content! Then the phone rang. In a matter of two or three minutes our contentment changed to restlessness, and my husband decided we had better catch the next plane home. For a short time we had experienced "circumstantial contentment," based solely on circumstances. Such contentment is always a temporary condition.

There is a "learned contentment," however, that

withstands the negative circumstances in life. Paul gives us an example when he says, "I have learned to be content whatever the circumstances" (Phil. 4:11). He was in jail, and the contentment he felt did not come naturally. He had to learn it.

NEGATIVE CAUSES OF RESTLESSNESS

The basic negative cause of restlessness can be labeled selfishness. When considerations, desires, and goals are focused on "self," a restless spirit will result. The restlessness found among women in the feminist movement arises from a philosophy based on self. With my attention focused on *my* rights, *my* control, *my* conditions, and *my* self, I cannot learn contentment.

It is helpful to examine Paul's attitudes as he sat in jail. He was not looking at his rights and focusing his attention on the dampness of the cell, the cobwebs, the mice, the stench, the lousy food, or mistreatment. His words from that prison were trying to encourage others in their attitudes, goals, and exaltation of the name of Jesus Christ.

Had Paul given in to the flesh and dwelt on himself and his circumstances he could never have written passages like Philippians 2:14, "Do everything without complaining or arguing, so that you may become blameless and pure"; or Philippians 4:6, "Do not be anxious about anything, but in everything, by prayer and petition, with thanksgiving, present your requests to God"; or Philippians 3:10, "I want to know Christ and the power of his resurrection and the fellowship of sharing in his sufferings, becoming like him in his death." Paul's attitudes were not selfish. Therefore he was able to learn contentment by showing concern for others and by giving thanks.

A passage from my husband's book *How to Manage Pressure Before Pressure Manages You* illustrates the importance of learning to be content whatever our circumstances.

"Your prison may be an overcrowded apartment with more children than bedrooms, an office without windows, a car that barely runs, or a job well beneath your ability and income needs. It may be an unhappy marriage or overly possessive parents. Whatever the privation or predicament, have you *learned* to be content? If not, you can never gain contentment by moving to a bigger apartment, getting a new job, or leaving your partner. Most people want to change their circumstances as a means to achieving peace. To the contrary, satisfaction is learned by developing a thanksgiving attitude where you are. Your present circumstances may not be Shangri-la, but they *are* your training ground. Since God wants to teach you contentment, learn your lesson as quickly as possible so He can speed you on to where He wants you to be. I am inclined to believe that many Christians spend their lives in the prison of discontentment because they refused to learn the lesson of satisfaction where they are."[1]

An inordinate perfectionist who develops the spirit of criticism will know little about contentment. This person tends to judge everything by her own standards and criticizes those who do not measure up to her.

Restlessness can be caused by lack of organization. When your affairs remain in constant disarray—unpaid bills, a messy house, unanswered mail, a cluttered office desk, or whatever—you begin to feel that things are out of control. This may be labeled as pressure, but it certainly results in restlessness. When life seems to be "out of control," it is necessary to regroup and reorganize priorities and seek God's wisdom for restoring order. Proverbs 3:6 tells us, "In all your ways acknowledge him, and he will make your paths straight."

POSITIVE RESULTS FROM RESTLESSNESS

Life is filled with hills and plateaus. According to Ecclesiastes 3:1, "There is a time for everything, and a season for every activity under heaven." We climb a hill to reach a goal, and then there is a plateau before we climb the next hill. God has a time and a plan for every event in our lives.

Ecclesiastes 3:2–4 tells us that there is "a time to be born and a time to die, a time to plant and a time to uproot, a time to kill and a time to heal, a time to tear down and a time to build."

God has often used a restlessness in my spirit to prepare me for the next hill to climb. He uses restlessness in the lives of Christians to help us focus attention on a new goal or a new plateau He wants us to reach. At other times, He uses restlessness in our hearts to guide us in determining His will in a given situation. As a Christian woman focuses on Christ and dwells on the Word of God, she can be sensitive to His message. When her heart is troubled and restless, it is wise for her to be still and determine what the Lord may be saying.

Two exciting challenges were presented to me as possibilities for Concerned Women for America. One was an offer to film an hour-long TV special that would be aired nationwide on prime-time television. The program seemed to be a marvelous way to educate women about the moral ills of our country and invite them to join Concerned Women for America so that together we could do something about it. Three days later I met with another group about the possibility of having a CWA National Convention in Washington, D.C., and transmitting it by closed-circuit television to between fifty and a hundred cities across the country. This challenge could also be used to educate and motivate American women to build a network of prayer and action.

Within three days I had been offered two fantastic opportunities to accomplish what I had dreamed of and prayed for. Some people said we should do both. I was open to God's will for CWA. I realized that for either venture to succeed would require a miracle filled with divine wisdom. There was no way I could accomplish either in my own wisdom and strength. God knew that I did not want to limit what He wanted to do and was capable of doing.

I set the decision aside for the weekend because we had company and a busy schedule. After the weekend I planned to sit down with all the information and try to list the pros and cons and seek God's will.

However, during the weekend my soul became troubled and restless as I thought about the TV special. In contrast, a spirit of contentment and excitement grew regarding the national satellite convention. By Monday I had in my mind a list that supported the convention and another list that discouraged the idea of a TV special. I believe the restlessness I experienced was God's way of moving me in the direction He wanted me to go. This kind of restlessness is blessed. It leads us in the right direction and brings contentment in the end. First Timothy 6:6 tells us, "But godliness with contentment is great gain."

NOTES

[1]Tim LaHaye, *How to Manage Pressure Before Pressure Manages You* (Grand Rapids: Zondervan, 1983), 151–52.

10.

Decisions That Produce Peace

The stacks of mail I receive from women carry different stories, but they repeat a basic theme. They ask, What is the woman's rightful place in the home and community? Hundreds of women have asked my husband and me that same question in person during our Family Life Seminars.

The answer depends on the individual woman, her energy level, her capabilities, her priorities, her responsibilities and, I might add, her husband's opinion on the matter.

Should mothers pursue full-time careers outside their homes? Unless a woman is divorced or widowed, I think it is far better for her family if she does not work full-time while her children are still at home and dependent on her. The stress involved may be too great for her to be an effective mother and wife and to enjoy life. The woman who has a full-time job outside the home doubles her workload. The truth is that most men are not emotionally inclined to assume the demanding task of running the household when a wife is pursuing a career. A man may feel that if his wife works, he's not a sufficient provider. This usually creates unnecessary tension between husband and wife.

After a woman pays for day care, transportation,

wardrobe, and other necessities, she adds only from 12 to 30 percent to the family income—yet she is now doing *twice* as much work. Her priority has also shifted from caring for the family to building a career. Her priority *must* be her relationship with God, then her husband and her children. When she gets these priorities out of line, she damages the fragile family structure and upsets the emotional climate of the home.

If a mother begins working outside the home for "self-fulfillment," the family very often begins to depend upon her income. Suddenly it's a "necessity" that she works. I believe a family should avoid the trap of having to depend on two paychecks for survival. With more money coming into the home, the desire for material things increases, and family members become addicted to having that extra money. Only under extreme circumstances would I recommend that a mother get a job outside of the home while her children are young.

I have had long talks on this subject with one of my daughters. She graduated from college and launched into a promising career as a teacher. After teaching for some time, she met her husband and they established a home. God has now given them their first child. Before marriage her major concern was doing the best job she could as a teacher. But when her "dream man" came along, the job became less important. And with the birth of a baby, the job became even less significant. Her top priority now is taking care of her husband and child.

I believe young motherhood is an "interlude" in a woman's life. It doesn't mean my daughter will never again be able to teach, but it does mean that she's voluntarily taken on a far more important responsibility at this time of her life as a wife and mother. She and her husband share the responsibility of training up their child to be a godly, civilized person. *This is no trivial task.* She's preparing a child to take his place in the world. The values she instills in him will affect everyone around him for the next seventy or eighty years.

They affect not only that family, but those in the community and the world.

What parents teach their children—or fail to teach them—will impinge on all those they come in contact with for their whole lives. In the study of the lives of mass murderers, dictators, or radical feminists, it becomes evident that their parents neglected to give them proper moral training. Because mothers and fathers abused or ignored their children, many youngsters have grown up with a desire to destroy the world around them.

We all have two basic needs in our lives: to love and be loved, and to feel that we have worth to ourselves and to others. Every child has these needs. During early years, when a child's moral values are forming, the parents are the primary agent in molding him and fulfilling these basic needs. Dr. William Glasser notes in *Reality Therapy,* "Learning to fulfill our needs must begin early in infancy and continue all our lives. If we fail to learn we will suffer, and this suffering always drives us to try unrealistic means to fulfill our needs. A person who does not learn as a little child to give and receive love may spend the rest of his life unsuccessfully trying to love."[1]

Glasser also observes, "When we cannot satisfy our total need for love, we will without fail suffer and react with many familiar psychological symptoms, from mild discomfort through anxiety and depression to complete withdrawal from the world around us."[2] During the early years of a child's life, I think it is very important that the mother remain available at home for him, providing him with what psychologists call "mother constancy." If the mother is a single parent who is left with no choice but to go to work, she should try to find a qualified "substitute mother" to care for her child during working hours.

In my earlier book, *I Am a Woman by God's Design,* I write, "If it is necessary to use a baby sitter or child-care center, the philosophy of either should be in agreement with what the child is taught in the home. Beliefs should be closely scrutinized in areas such as God, discipline, truthfulness, morals, authority, clean language, consistency of promises, standards of obedience, and so forth. This idea is not as farfetched as it may seem. I have had young mothers come to me, with great concern, because their two- and three-year-olds picked up four-letter words from the child-care center where they were enrolled. They will eventually hear these words in school and maybe even try them out, but a school that agrees with you on these issues is preferable to one where the teacher has no conscience about them. The teacher should reinforce your training and cooperate with you."[3]

Once a child begins attending school, I believe the mother has more options available to her outside of the home—options far more important than simply earning a paycheck. If a mother wishes to work part-time, she should plan to be at home when her children return from school. This is one way that her part-time job does not become her top priority.

To be honest, I think a Christian woman would be far wiser to use her time in ministry work or in acquiring some valuable skills to use in the event of her husband's death. If acquiring more income creates an appetite in the woman for materialism rather than assisting with the immediate needs of her family, then I suggest that she not let herself be tempted. I think it is presumptuous not to prepare wisely for the future.

If a woman has spare time at home, she might consider using her talents to help others. She can get involved in local church outreaches; lead a Bible study; teach a Sunday school class; share the gospel with neighbors; offer her services to a local pregnancy crisis home for unwed mothers; visit and encourage the elderly in rest homes. There are battered women (maybe even Christian women) who need to be tenderly loved and cared for. Or she can get involved in any of a number of Christian women's organizations such as Concerned Women for America.

If the woman is a believer in Jesus Christ, then she must realize that one of the most important jobs she can perform is to pray for her country, for her political and religious leaders. She can pray for her church and for the souls of those who don't know Christ. Praying does not give worldly status or recognition, but it does change things. It is a great satisfaction for both men and women to see their prayers answered.

SINGLE WOMEN

Single women have some important decisions to make about their lives in the context of restlessness. When I counsel singles, I'm often asked, "Should I plan for a career?" I always tell them: "Of course, you should. You'd be unwise not to plan for the future." Many single women who wish to marry think they should simply wait around for the right man to come into their lives. But they don't know what the future will bring. They may never marry. A single woman should get an education and develop whatever skills the Lord has given her. If she desires a husband, she should ask the Lord to provide one if that is His will.

In the meantime, she should plan to get involved in a ministry where she will be contributing to the needs of others. It may be God's will for her to remain single and serve the Lord. If so, she'll be able to devote all her energies to His work without being torn between family responsibilities and what may be a clear call from God.

WHICH WAY ARE YOU GOING?

If you are a restless woman, you're in transition. Which way are you going? Are you looking forward to living in an asexual culture, where men and women are expected to perform the same duties? Or would you prefer to get back to basics—living an effective and influential life at home, training your own children, and being cared for and loved by your husband? Do you wish to affirm your own femininity and fulfill your worth as a woman according to God's will? Or is it your desire to reject your natural character traits, demand your rights, and become more masculine in your behavior and attitudes? The choice is yours.

If you're in transition back to basic morality, then you have some work to do. Whether you're single or married, you can't remain neutral over the serious issues facing all of us. You can't remain neutral as the family is destroyed; you can't remain silent while thousands of unborn babies are destroyed every day; you can't remain uninvolved over the increasing drug abuse in our society; you can't be passive in the face of child abuse and neglect. Your silence may in essence express approval of these things.

Obviously you aren't expected to do everything. You will have to consider prayerfully what God may want you to get involved in. Jesus did not tell us, "Go thou and do *everything.*"

I think both the world and our churches expect too much of women today.. We cannot possibly be political leaders, homemakers, lovers, mothers, Bible study leaders, charity workers, and career professionals—all at one time. Few women can adequately fill all these roles.

The image of the "supermom" is misleading. A woman who tries to handle a career, is involved in a church, cares for her home and children, is a good friend to those in need, and responds to every crisis that arises will probably be driven to an early grave. You and I can't do everything. We must depend on the Lord to show us what *He* wants us to do with our time. We should not be driven by guilt feelings or the sense that we're somehow obligated to be involved in every worthwhile activity. Just because you see a need does not necessarily mean the Lord expects *you* to fulfill it.

As a member of the body of Christ, you have an

obligation to seek God's will for your life—both in your homemaking and in leisure times.

MAKING CHOICES

What you wish to do with your life is in your hands. Even if you're a Christian, you can resist the working of the Holy Spirit in your life. You can go your own way, striving to solve life's problems in your own strength. You can focus your attention on self rather than others and develop a selfish attitude toward life. On the other hand, if you simply commit all of your problems—finances, family conflicts, spirituality—to the Lord, He will work out the difficulties in your life. Are you in transition back to Christian morality, or are you drifting toward selfish feminism? The choice is yours.

If you are not a believer in Jesus Christ, you're facing a terrible dilemma in this life. If you're restless with the life you've been leading, if you think you've gotten a bad deal in your marriage, if you think that your financial problems are unsolvable, I have an answer for you: Confess your need for a Savior to Jesus Christ; confess your sins and ask Him to become the Lord of your life. Give your struggles to Him, and He will give you wisdom and guidance as you face any problems you may be going through right now. Your restlessness can begin to change to contentment.

To become a believer in Jesus Christ is the most important transition a woman or man can make in life. It is a transition that transforms! If you respond with a confession of your need for a Savior and ask to have your sins forgiven, you will begin a transition from the restless, selfish life to a transformed life with purpose and direction. If Jesus Christ truly is the Son of God (as I believe He is), then He has some important things to say to all of us—about our dilemmas, our personal relationships, our ultimate reason for living, and basic principles for living a godly life in this secular humanistic world.

If the feminist leaders whom we have reviewed in this book would bow their knees before God and invite Him to be their Lord and Savior, they too could experience this transformation.

Obedience to God does not produce selfishness or restlessness. On the contrary, abiding peace and contentment result from obeying the principles for living in God's Word. Remember this promise from God: "You will keep in perfect peace him whose mind is steadfast, because he trusts in you" (Isaiah 26:3).

NOTES

[1] William Glasser, *Reality Therapy* (New York: Harper & Row, 1975), 13.

[2] Ibid., 11.

[3] Beverly LaHaye, *I Am a Woman by God's Design* (Old Tappan, N.J.: Fleming H. Revell, 1980), 4.

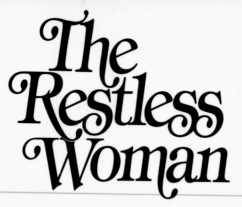

The Restless Woman

Who is the "restless woman"?

She is a woman who, in the author's words, "has been 'liberated' from traditional roles, yet now finds herself feeling empty and without goals; she's *any* woman who is uneasy and dissatisfied with her lot in life." And the closer she seems to get to her goal of satisfaction, the further it recedes into the distance.

Moreover, the restless woman is caught in the middle of a political and religious battleground not of her making. On one side are the activists agitating for radical social change in every area of our lives; on the other side are the forces of traditionalism in morality and lifestyle. The restless woman is caught without sufficient spiritual or ideological weapons with which to defend herself. She bears the brunt of instability in our society.

Beverly LaHaye has found that this restlessness can be turned into a positive force. This book explores the personal and social roots of restlessness and suggests ways out of the dilemma. The author focuses on making choices—about career, about family, about roles—and shows how obedience to God is the ultimate means to gaining peace and contentment for living. And the ultimate means to finding a woman's rightful place in the home and in the community.

Beverly LaHaye has counseled thousands of women through Family Life Seminars, as co-host of the weekly television program "The LaHayes on Family Life," and as the founder of Concerned Women for America. Among her other books is *I Am a Woman by God's Design*.

0

25986 27091

a ZONDERVAN PUBLICATION

18337p
ZONDERVAN BOOKS
RELIGION/WOMEN'S ISSUES
ISBN 0-310-27091-X